Celebrating the Game

Photographs from the Bereswill Collection at the Hockey Hall of Fame

Andrew Podnieks

HOCKEY HALL *of* FAME

Library and Archives Canada Cataloguing in Publication

Podnieks, Andrew
    Celebrating the game : photographs from the Bereswill collection at the Hockey
Hall of Fame / Andrew Podnieks in association with the Hockey Hall of Fame.

ISBN 978-1-55168-283-9
ISBN 1-55168-283-4

    1. National Hockey League—Pictorial works. 2. Hockey—History—Pictorial works.
3. Hockey players—Pictorial works. 4. Bereswill, Paul J.—Photograph collections.
5. Hockey Hall of Fame—Photograph collections. 6. Photograph collections—Ontario—
Toronto. I. Bereswill, Paul J. II. Hockey Hall of Fame III. Title.

GV847.8.N3P57 2006   796.962'640222   C2006-903770-1

We acknowledge the financial support of
the Government of Canada through
the Book Publishing Industry
Development Program (BPIDP)
for our publishing activities.

Celebrating the Game

Photographs from the Bereswill Collection at the Hockey Hall of Fame

Andrew Podnieks

HOCKEY HALL *of* FAME

FENN

Fenn Publishing Company Ltd.

Bolton, Ontario

Contents

Foreword
by Pat LaFontaine

Just a few days after I was inducted into the Hockey Hall of Fame in November 2003, the New York Islanders graciously offered to recognize this accomplishment with a special night in my honour. The club brought in former GM Bill Torrey to welcome my family and me to the Nassau Coliseum ice. They prepared a wonderful video highlight of my time in an Islanders uniform and that helped bring a flood of memories home.

As I gazed at the crowd filling the old arena, my attention was caught by a familiar figure hiding behind a camera near the Zamboni entrance. Paul Bereswill's presence at another important event in my life reminded me how my career had come full circle.

I was a naïve 17-year-old playing for Verdun in the Quebec Junior League when I first met Paul. He had been given the assignment by his editors at *Sports Illustrated* to fly into Montreal and capture images of this new hockey "phenom"—an American kid setting records in the league made famous by Guy Lafleur and Gilbert Perreault.

I was billeting with the Boyer family on Champlain Boulevard in Verdun when Paul first came calling. This being my first official photo shoot for a major magazine, I had no idea what to expect. Long before he ever took out his camera, we just sat and talked. I was impressed that he first took a keen interest in me as a person. He wanted to know about my family and what it was like growing up on Williams Lake in Michigan.

He showed a great deal of compassion for the pressures I was under and we discussed which NHL team might draft me and determine where I'd spend the next few years of my life. When Paul finally got around to taking some pictures, it was easy to see why he was considered a "pro's pro."

Athletes are often credited with having great hand-eye coordination and the great ones are acclaimed for their "feel" of the game. But few players I ever skated with had as great a feel for the game as Paul Bereswill. The *Sports Illustrated* spread came out fantastic thanks to his expertise.

A few months later, I was drafted by the Stanley Cup champion Islanders. It was no small coincidence that the team played in Paul's backyard in Uniondale, Long Island. During my days on the Island, it seemed that Paul was present for every major event. He covered the Olympics, and we had even more time to reflect on our mutual good fortune to be on such a grand international stage. He always was quick to share a story of his son, Jason, and when my wife and I started our family, Paul and I compared notes on child-raising.

I've often heard that you don't always remember what people say or do, but you always remember how they make you feel. Paul has a heart that is as big as his talent with a shutter and a lens. He always offers his assistance when it comes to helping with my charity, The Companions in Courage Foundation. It's one thing to be a great photographer; it's quite another to be so generous and giving.

I am honoured to be asked to make a small contribution to this great collection of work by my friend. Paul's images capture one of the great eras in hockey history. His feel for the moment sets him apart from his peers and makes this work an absolute collector's item.

I consider it a privilege to have been blessed with the ability to play the game I love at the highest level for 15 years. Paul was performing at an elite level long before I ever strapped on a pair of NHL skates, and he continues to be one of the best at capturing the beauty, artistry, and aggressiveness of our great game long after I have retired.

Sitting beside my desk is that photo that Paul took of me and my family on the Nassau Coliseum ice in November 2003. It's beautiful in its simplicity, yet it captures a moment in time that I will cherish the rest of my life. How many of the images in this wonderful collection will YOU cherish?

Pat LaFontaine
August 2006

Brent Ashton

Most every hockey career starts out the same, and it's only after a bit of time that each defines itself, takes on its own personality, becomes a small chapter in the NHL's long and distinguished history.

For Brent Ashton, the beginning came in Vancouver. After playing all of his junior hockey in his hometown of Saskatoon, he was drafted by the Canucks in 1979. His brother, Ron, had played for the Winnipeg Jets in the WHA, and now younger brother Brent was making his way to the big tent, as it were.

Brent got to his first training camp as a 19-year-old and played well enough that he made the team. He had size, skill with the puck, and defensive smarts, and the team needed a left winger. He played half a season as a rookie, scoring just five goals, and the year after, a full season, he had 18 goals, not bad at all.

Then things started to go a little off the rails. In the summer of 1981, he was sent to the Jets because the Canucks had signed free agent Ivan Hlinka. He was part of what was then equal compensation, the team losing a free agent getting a player of like value from the signing club. The Jets turned around and traded Ashton to the Colorado Rockies just a few hours later. Okay, no big deal. So, Ashton went to camp that fall in Denver, and scored 24 goals on an awful team. The Rockies were losing money, however, so the franchise moved to New Jersey for the '82-'83 season and Ashton followed. His production dipped, though, and the then "Mickey Mouse" team sent him to Minnesota just days before the start of the '83-'84 season.

The North Stars utilized Ashton as a checker and fourth liner, and his offensive numbers fell accordingly. At 23 years old, with his fourth franchise in five years, he was now scoring seven goals in a year. The season after started poorly for him, so Ashton was traded to Quebec. Seldom before has the term "change of scenery" been as healthily valid as in his case. In half a season with the Nordiques, Ashton scored 27 goals playing a regular shift and the power play.

The next year started out just as well. He had 25 goals in the first 46 games, but now the Nordiques were offering him as trade bait—as a scorer. Detroit bit, and acquired Ashton in a multi-player deal. He ended '86-'87 scoring 15 times for the Red Wings, giving him 40 goals in 78 games with the two teams over the full season. Detroit made it to the Conference finals before losing to the mighty Oilers, so clearly he was a contributing factor to the team's success.

Ashton chipped in 26 goals all of the following year, and again the team went to the Conference finals. In the off season, though, he was traded straight up to Winnipeg for Paul MacLean, and it was there that he settled for the next four years. He later was traded to Boston (two years) and Calgary, in 1992-93, at the end of his career.

In all, the totals are amazing: nine NHL teams, 998 total regular-season games, 284 goals. Ashton was traded eight times in deals involving a total of 16 players. It was one of the strangest NHL odysseys in the league's history, but a wonderful one at that.

Kjell Dahlin & Mats Naslund

When Mats Naslund signed with the Montreal Canadiens to play in 1982-83 at age 22, he became the first European-trained player to join the vaunted bleu, blanc, et rouge. When he got to his first NHL training camp, some players thought his appearance was something of a joke because at 5'6" and 160 pounds, he was hardly the kind of player who was likely to make an impact in the ever-enlarging NHL.

How wrong were the critics! Not only did Naslund earn a place in the lineup, he earned more than his fair share of ice time and scored 26 goals and 71 points in that first season. Not bad for a supposed squirt. The year after, he had 29 goals, and then he exploded. Naslund had played the first four years of his pro career in Sweden, where the league schedule was 50 games on bigger ice with less physical play. After two years in the NHL, he had learned the North American game and made the necessary adjustments, and in '84-'85 he led the team with 42 goals.

His great season, and his ability to play in the league despite his size, encouraged the Canadiens to sign another Swede, Kjell Dahlin. Dahlin grew up on the same street as Naslund in Timra, and he had just finished his requisite military duty as an anti-aircraft gunner. He came to Montreal's camp in 1985 and had a phenomenal year gunning goals, the two Swedes integral in the team's surprise Stanley Cup victory.

Dahlin played on a line with Bobby Smith, and by season's end the newcomer led all NHL rookies with 71 points (32 goals). He had a great wrist shot and was a perfect compliment to Smith, and on another line Naslund had a career best 43 goals and 110 points. Naslund averaged a point a game in the playoffs, but Dahlin tapered off badly. He managed just four goals in the final 19 regular season games and just two more in the entire playoffs. He admitted fatigue was the only problem.

Used to that 50-game season back in Sweden, by the time all was said and done Dahlin played twice as long in '85-'86, but he did score one big goal in the Cup finals. Dahlin netted the game winner in the third game to give the Habs a 2-1 series lead, a lead they never relinquished. Naslund had two goals and an assist in that 5-3 win over Calgary. He also scored a key overtime goal in an earlier series against Quebec and was a force in the playoffs just as he had been in the regular season.

Naslund continued to be a star with Montreal for the next four years. Although he never had another 43-goal season and never reached 100 points again, he was still a reliable scorer, a hard and consistent worker, and a great team player. Dahlin played just two more years, both shortened by knee injuries. He continued to find the schedule and travel difficult and returned to Sweden in 1988, but for one magical year the two Swedes were sensational in helping Montreal win a Stanley Cup.

Wayne Gretzky & Joey Moss

Bobby Orr used to visit Boston-area hospitals to cheer up the patients, usually sick kids. He did so quietly, without photographers and reporters, and when he said good-bye to the kids and headed to the rink, he said he felt like the luckiest person alive.

Wayne Gretzky and the amazing Oilers of the 1980s, for all their lightning speed, incredible talent, and sublime skill, were inspired by a kid named Joey Moss in the dressing room. He was the brother of Vicki Moss, girlfriend of Gretzky for seven years. Joey was born with Down syndrome, and in an early autobiography Gretzky wrote, "We players were given certain talents at birth, and Joey had some taken at birth. Who's to say I didn't get what he lost?" That was the perspective that helped the Oilers achieve all they managed in those amazing 1980s.

Joey wasn't blessed with all the physical ability in the world, but he performed his simple dressing room duties like folding towels and vacuuming with Stanley Cup determination. He was with the Oilers in the winter and the local Eskimos in the CFL in the summer. He started as a 21-year-old, and today he still mans the room, high-fiving the players as they leave for the ice or enter after coming off the ice after every period and game.

When Joey first arrived on the scene, he was taken under the wing of trainer Lyle Kulchisky who gave him small chores at first and then more important ones with time. Joey was the twelfth of 13 children, shy and reserved as a kid, but when he joined the Oilers he became an extrovert. Now, the players simply call him a celebrity. He is known as the honourary commissioner of the Oilers' training camp, and at the end of camp the winning intra-squad team is awarded the Joey Moss Cup. In 2003, he was given the Seventh Man Award by the NHL, a tribute to his contributions to the team and, indeed, to the game.

The Gretzky-Joey relationship is a lifelong one. Gretzky helped him get that first job back in the early Oilers' days, and they lived together for a short time when Gretzky was an Edmonton bachelor. Gretzky had an aunt who was also afflicted by Down, so he well knew the challenges of the illness and also the unimportance of it to being a quality person. When Gretzky was traded to Los Angeles in 1988, he asked owner Peter Pocklington for a personal pledge to make sure Joey was okay, and years later when the Oilers retired number 99, right there beside him at centre ice was Joey Moss. He never scored any goals or made any great passes for the Oilers on ice, but his perseverance, friendship, and commitment to the team were priceless contributions nonetheless.

Jacques Demers

Hockey: 1993 Stanley Cup
Montreal Canadiens Head Coach
Jacques Demers holding trophy

In the fall of 2005, Jacques Demers released his autobiography, ironically titled *Jacques Demers En Toutes Lettres* (or, *Jacques Demers from A to Z*) in which he revealed the shocking news that he could not read or write. A grown man of 60-plus years, he had accomplished virtually everything a coach could wish—yet he could not read or write. Unfathomable.

Born in Montreal, Demers lived under a brutally violent father who terrified the family. As a result, young Jacques was too anxious to learn, too scared to do anything but survive. Yet by the time he was a 30-year-old man he was hired by the Indianapolis Racers to coach the WHA team. He moved on to Quebec and the NHL and later had long stops in St. Louis and Detroit. His teams usually had .500 records and made the playoffs, but he didn't achieve great fame until 1992-93, his first year as coach of his native Montreal Canadiens.

That season, the team went on a surprise run to the Stanley Cup, led by goalie Patrick Roy and ten overtime wins during the grueling playoff run. Demers ended his career in Tampa Bay and then worked for French-language radio in Montreal. All the while he couldn't read or write to save his life.

When he coached in the U.S., he explained that his English was too poor to handle contracts or scouting reports. When he returned home, he said his French was rusty from years of neglect. He hired assistants to worry about contracts. He kept copious notes near him to give the impression of a busy note-taker. He spoke well enough to be literate, by all appearances. Yet at no time could he actually read the newspaper or write a speech for a dinner.

His children didn't know of his situation. His wife knew only because she complained about being in charge of paying the bills all the time and he was forced to tell her. None of his players knew, and when Demers revealed his truth, they came to his defence, both by being supportive of his skills as a coach and his bravery in revealing such a secret.

His was a handicap brilliantly disguised, like the hero/heroine of M. Butterfly or Cyrano de Bergerac wooing his love through the face and voice of a friend. Demers was there, but he wasn't. He knew his hockey—he still does—but he couldn't articulate any more than was needed to run a practice or change lines during a game. He was embarrassed and ashamed by his problem, but he wasn't going to let it ruin his life. He rightly pointed out that no one would have hired an illiterate to run an NHL team. That would be foolish.

Of course, this doesn't mean the league will ever hire an illiterate knowingly, but that it did on several occasions with several teams suggests that hockey smarts and book smarts are not necessarily connected.

Pat LaFontaine

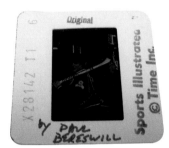

The man behind the numbers was so much more than the various lines of statistics that comprise the career of Pat LaFontaine. However, one number is worth its weight in gold. February 22, 1980, was doubly important for LaFontaine. It was the day of his 15th birthday, and it was the day, to celebrate that natal date, he sat in front of the television and watched Team USA beat the Soviet Union 4-3 in the Miracle on Ice at the Olympics in Lake Placid. That was one of those days he looked to most especially for inspiration as he followed his dream of playing in the NHL.

LaFontaine, born in St. Louis but a longtime resident of Detroit, pursued his dream in a very non-traditional way for American players of his era. The 17-year-old went off and played junior hockey in Quebec. He told his parents he wanted three years to play with the best juniors around. If he wasn't successful, he'd come home and go to university. Two years later, he was in the NHL.

More amazing, his only season of junior with Verdun was 1982-83 when he recorded remarkable numbers. In 70 games, he scored 104 goals and 234 points, an average of more than three points a game for the entire season. Rather than trade in on this and turn pro, LaFontaine decided to spend the next year with the USA National Team and play at the '84 Olympics. Only then did he join the New York Islanders, the team that had drafted him in the summer of 1983.

At the end of that '83-'84 season, he helped the Isles to their fifth straight Stanley Cup finals, but they came up short against the burgeoning Edmonton Oilers. The next year, the full-time rookie scored 19 goals. The year after, he hit 30, then 38, then 47. LaFontaine had six straight seasons of 40 goals or more, peaking at 54 in '89-'90.

LaFontaine spent eight years with the Islanders as one of the lynchpins of their offence. In 1991, though, he asked to be traded and the Buffalo Sabres were more than happy to accommodate. He scored 99 goals in his first 141 games with his new team, but early in the '93-'94 season he suffered a serious knee injury that kept him off ice for a year and a half.

When he returned, he won the Bill Masterton Trophy for his perseverance, and he played with the same old offensive power. A worse injury befell him, though, on October 17, 1996, another date he won't soon forget. He took an elbow to the head and suffered a serious concussion, so serious that not only did he miss almost another year but the Sabres didn't want him back for fear of contributing to a possibly more serious injury.

Again, though, the player persevered. He started fresh with the New York Rangers, in '97-'98, but just when things looked like everything would be fine, they weren't. LaFontaine played 67 games and scored 23 goals, but in that 67th game he suffered another concussion. This time he called it quits, but by that time his 15-year pro career had been meaningful enough that he had no regrets form carrying on as long as he had— and no regrets about leaving with his future health intact.

Pelle Lindbergh

Per-Erik (Pelle) Lindbergh died a horrible death, suffering tragic injuries as a result of a car crash on November 10, 1985. But before he passed away, he left his mark on the world of hockey, most notably in Philadelphia where he played all of his brief NHL career.

Lindbergh first came to prominence at the 1979 World Championship in Moscow. Flyers' scout Larry Melnyk regarded him highly, but so did everyone else. In fact, the NHL's Central Scouting ranked Lindbergh as the best available goalie in the world for the upcoming draft. The Flyers made him the second goalie chosen, after Atlanta took Pat Riggin, but Lindbergh didn't come to Philadelphia right away.

He spent the next season playing again in Sweden in order that he could represent Tre Kronor in the Olympics, and the year after he played for Maine in the AHL, the Flyers' farm team, where he was named both rookie of the year and league MVP. Lindbergh made his NHL debut in '81-'82, but it was the year after that he made a breakthrough and established himself as the team's number-one goalie. That rookie season went from great to bad for Lindbergh, though. He was named to play in the All-Star Game in February 1983, but the experience was anything but all-star-like for the young goalie.

In the first place, he was injured in January and got into only one game before the All-Star Game. Also, just before the glamour game, his Flyers' teammates gave him a "rookie haircut" which upset him more than made him feel part of the team. And lastly, he expected to play like an all-star with a group of players intent on winning, unaware that the game was usually a very loose and casual affair. As a result, there was little defence in the game and he surrendered a record seven goals in his 30 minutes of action. Four of those were scored by Wayne Gretzky in the third period, an achievement that was an All-Star Game record, and many close to Lindbergh said it took him more than a year to regain his confidence after that game.

But regain it he did, in spades. In 1984-85, Lindbergh was the best goalie in the NHL, hands down. He played more games than any other netminder (65), more minutes (3,858), and won more games (40). He played in the All-Star Game again and performed admirably, and at season's end he was named winner of the Vezina Trophy.

Early the next year, the expectations for the rising star high, Lindbergh was killed in a car crash. The team had put together a ten-game unbeaten streak and everything looked rosy for Lindbergh and his girlfriend, Kerstin Pietzsch. Back home, he had also recently starred in a movie called *Don't Leave Me Alone*, and he was Sweden's most popular athlete after the great tennis star, Bjorn Borg.

Despite the horrible accident, the life of Lindbergh was not a waste. Just days after he was laid to rest, John Keeler of Northfield, New Jersey, came back to life. Keeler, 51, had been told by doctors his heart was giving out and his life was coming to an end. Lindbergh's parents allowed doctors to remove their son's vital organs from his body. Keeler ended up receiving the heart of the 26-year-old Pelle Lindbergh, and so in death the goalie made the finest save of his career—off ice. His heart still beats inside another man, a man grateful for a second life, even though it came at the expense of a life too briefly lived.

Scotty Bowman

To steal from Rodney Dangerfield, if you look the word "coach" up in the dictionary, it says, "someone who is hired to be fired." Yet in a profession where five years is an eternity and ninety-nine per cent of coaches don't survive that long, Scotty Bowman is without compare. He started the year of expansion—original expansion, that is, in 1967—and continued past the 21st century. There was one season when he didn't coach because he was Buffalo's general manager (1980-81), and there were four more years of retirement (1987-91) which evidently weren't particularly fulfilling because he returned in 1991 and coached for more than a decade again.

People are born to coach only as a second choice, a backup plan, an alternative. Bowman, special as he was, was no different. He played junior hockey in Quebec before an injury ended his dreams of playing in the NHL, but once he started behind the bench he was a natural. In 30 years as a coach, he had a losing record in the regular season exactly once. Here's the funny thing: that sub-.500 record came in 1986-87 in Buffalo when he was 3-7-2 in the team's first dozen games, hardly a measure of even brief failure in a career that spanned more than 2,100 games!

He started with the Montreal Canadiens under San Pollock, but Bowman's first big break—like so many players—came in 1967 when the league doubled in size from six teams to twelve. He took over the St. Louis Blues, and for three successive years guided the Blues to the Stanley Cup finals.

True enough, they lost every year—didn't win a game, in fact—but they were always playing one of the Original Six teams, stocked with talent and accumulated wisdom from being around for some forty years or more.

Bowman's second big break was to inherit the coaching duties of those Canadiens under whom he had first cut his teeth. He started in 1971-72, and in eight years with the Habs he won five Stanley Cups. He then spent eight years with Buffalo, seven as a coach as well as GM, and it was there he had his "worst" record. That is, he didn't win a Stanley Cup, but he missed the playoffs only once, his last full year with the Sabres.

Bowman went to Pittsburgh to work in player development, but when coach Bob Johnson passed away suddenly, he took over behind the bench through this most difficult period. The Penguins won the Cup in 1991-92 under Bowman, and the next year he coached as well before moving on to the Motor City.

The Detroit Red Wings hired him in the summer of 1993. It was an interesting challenge for Bowman. The Wings last won the Cup in 1955, but they had an owner, Mike Ilitch, who was willing to do whatever it took to bring the Cup back. In part, that meant spending money; in part it meant hiring smart people to spend that money wisely. Bowman was a significant piece of the puzzle, and by the time he retired for good in 2002, he had, indeed, brought the Cup back to Detroit—three times, in fact.

None of Bowman's records are remotely within reach. His 1,244 regular-season wins and 223 playoff wins will take decades of success to equal, and his most remarkable achievement—nine Stanley Cups—might fall into the category of untouchable, right beside Glenn Hall's 502 consecutive appearances by a goalie or Wayne Gretzky's 2,857 career points.

Walt Poddubny

Injuries and inconsistency were the biggest reasons why Walt Poddubny didn't make it as far or for as long as he might have in the NHL, but he still had a fine career in which he scored 40 goals one season, 38 goals twice, and 28 goals as a rookie.

Known as a huge fan and collector of Three Stooges videos and memorabilia, Poddubny brought a loosey-goosey attitude to the rink, an attitude that couldn't but help develop a fledgling career that saw him oft-injured as he started to earn his keep in the NHL. He was drafted by Edmonton in 1980 but was traded to the Leafs two years later, and it was with the Leafs that he fought to establish himself in the league.

In his first full season, '82-'83, he played on a line with Miroslav Frycer and Peter Ihnacak, and the left winger responded with 28 goals. He had missed most of the previous season with a broken ankle. The year after his outbreak rookie season, he hurt his knee and broke his thumb, played only 38 games and scored just eleven goals. The next two years were more of the same, but he was demoted to the AHL farm team for long stretches both seasons. In '85-'86, though, he scored almost a goal a game with the St. Catharines Saints and seemed to have found his form again.

By the summer of 1986, though, the Leafs weren't sure what they were investing in—a top flight NHLer or superstar minor leaguer—so they traded him to the Rangers where rookie GM Phil Esposito took him under his wing. Esposito ensured Poddubny played centre, not wing, and he told the player to worry about scoring, not defence. The result was a career year for Poddubny. He led the Blueshirts in scoring with 40 goals and 87 points playing on a line with Tomas Sandstrom and Jan Erixon, two Europeans, just as he had in Toronto.

The next year, Poddubny played on a line with Hall of Famer Marcel Dionne (back on left wing) and right winger Lucien Deblois. Again he had another great year (38 goals, 88 points), but the team missed the playoffs. As a result, he was part of a big trade with the Quebec Nordiques which saw himself, Jari Gronstrand, Bruce Bell, and a 4th-round draft choice in 1989 (Eric Dubois) head to the Nordiques as Jason Lafreniere and Normand Rochefort headed to Broadway.

To prove his New York years were no fluke, Poddubny scored 38 goals again in his third successive, injury-free season. Despite this season, though, the Nordiques, going through a bad stretch, missed the playoffs again and Poddubny was traded, this time to New Jersey. Poddubny played three part-time years in the Meadowlands, headed overseas at the end of his career, and then returned to North America to begin a career in coaching. In all, he played 468 games and had 422 points, perfectly fine numbers for any Stooges fan.

Bobby Carpenter

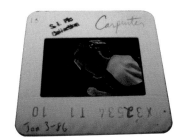

In so many ways, the best of Bobby Carpenter was also the worst. The Massachusetts native was such a star in high school at St. John's Prep in that state that for the 1981 draft he was slated to be selected among the first few selections. Carpenter was hoping to be chosen by Hartford, which had the fourth overall pick, so he could live close to home, but at the last minute Washington made a deal with Colorado for the third overall selection and the Caps selected Carpenter instead.

Carpenter's father was furious, but money spoke louder than words in the family and the Caps offered the 18-year-old a multi-year deal at about $600,000 a year, colossal numbers at the time. Dale Hawerchuk was the first overall selection that year, and time has proved that Hartford's fourth pick—Ron Francis—was no slouch, either!

The "Can't Miss Kid," as *Sports Illustrated* dubbed Carpenter, went to his first training camp and made the team. But, as the highest-ever drafted American-born player the expectations for him were every bit as large as the contract he signed. Carpenter's first five seasons were the best of his 18-year career, and one, 1984-85, stood out as spectacular.

As a rookie, he had an excellent introduction to the league, scoring 32 goals and 67 total points. The year after his numbers were almost identical (32 goals and 69 points). Year three he was right there again when he recorded 68 points, but by now it seemed his mature years weren't going to launch him into the superstar status of Gretzky, Messier, or Hawerchuk. Still, a second-tier star was nothing to be ashamed of.

Carpenter started '84-'85 by playing for USA at the 1984 Canada Cup. That team was eliminated by Sweden in the semi-finals, and Carpenter went on to score 53 goals, the best single season by any U.S.-born player in NHL history. If he never played another game, he had made his mark on the American hockey scene. Rather than build on that great season, however, the confident Carpenter immediately went into aggressive mode with the Capitals and spent the summer embroiled in a contract dispute. He signed a new deal prior to the '85-'86 season, though, but then had an average year by his high standards, scoring just 56 points.

The next year, he and coach Bryan Murray didn't get along. Murray cut the player's ice time, and Carpenter responded by playing evermore poorly. Before Christmas, Carpenter was relegated to the press box until he could be traded, but when he was sent to the Rangers he lacked the inspiration of his early years.

Over the next 12 years, he remained in the NHL, playing with four teams over that time. His best years came with Boston where he scored 25 goals twice. By the time he got to New Jersey in 1993, the elder Carpenter was a role player, but he was playing on a team that was on the upswing. Ironically, his worst statistical year was '94-'95, but it was the year he won his only Stanley Cup, with the Devils.

After such a long wait, after the pressure of his teenage years and the expectations of his prime years, winning the Cup under such relaxed circumstances was fitting reward for the high draft choice back in 1981.

Daryl Evans

It's now known simply as the Miracle on Manchester. The Manchester refers to the street name on which sat the Los Angeles Forum. The Miracle refers to the greatest comeback in playoff history. The hero of that night was Daryl Evans.

It was the first round of the playoffs, a best-of-five affair in 1982, and the mighty Edmonton Oilers met the Los Angeles Kings in a matchup that was as lop-sided as they got at that time of year. During the regular season the Oilers finished with 48 wins and 111 points. The Kings? Try 24 wins and 63 points. They were literally half as successful as the Oilers were over a full season. Wayne Gretzky led the league with 212 points, the first time in league history a player had reached 200 points. Yet also among the leaders were Kings veteran Marcel Dionne (50 goals and 117 points) and linemate Dave Taylor (106 points).

Nonetheless, there was no sane hockey prognosticator who would have given the Kings a chance in this series. In the first game, however, Los Angeles managed a ridiculous and sloppy win by the score of 10-8. The Oilers had to fight to win game two, 3-2 in overtime, and in game three they were finding their top gear and pouring on the power. Midway through the game they led 5-0, and the romp was on. Or, so it seemed.

Then a strange thing happened. The Kings scored to make it 5-1, then again to make it 5-2. They added another and another and finally the tying goal to send the game into overtime, and in the extra period Evans scored on Grant Fuhr to give the Kings a most improbable 6-5 win and 2-1 series lead. The Kings lost the next game by 3-2 again, but in the deciding game they simply pulled away from the Oilers, 7-4. The cocky and mighty Stanley Cup favourites were sent home after a horrible opening-round series.

Surprisingly, Evans didn't go very far in the NHL. He was a scorer wherever he went after converting from defence to forward as a junior, but this ability earned him very few chances to prove himself at the top level because scouts thought he was too small for the big NHL game. In these 1982 playoffs, he had five goals and 13 points in ten games, and the next year he managed just 18 goals over 80 games of the regular season. It was his only significant time in the league. Next year, despite scoring 51 goals in the AHL, he played just four games with the Kings. He ended up going to Washington and finally Toronto, but in neither city did he play more than a few games. Still, he remained a solid scorer in the AHL until retiring.

After hanging up his skates, Evans landed a job at a car dealership in Los Angeles for seven years (1992-99), also working the Kings games as a colour commentator. Ironically, during this time Gretzky came to the Kings and took the team to the Cup finals in 1993 for the first time in team history, a year after eliminating those same Oilers in another exciting Kings-Oilers series. For one year Evans was director of special ticket sales at the new Staples Centre. He then became hockey director at a training centre in California and has become the president of the Los Angeles Kings alumni association.

Wayne Gretzky

It was a strange blip in the career of Wayne Gretzky those 18 regular-season games plus another 13 in the 1996 playoffs. At the time, it all made sense. Looking back, it's hard to picture the Great One in a St. Louis sweater at all.

The 1995-96 season was a turning point for Los Angeles. The Kings had missed the playoffs the previous year, the lockout-shortened season, and in '95-'96, Gretzky was in his eighth year with the team and in the final year of his contract. The man who had orchestrated the most amazing trade in league history, Kings owner Bruce McNall, was on his way to jail for fraud, and Gretzky's loyalty to the team seemed more tenuous than ever. Gretzky and McNall were fast friends, co-owners of the Toronto Argonauts with John Candy and co-purchasers of the most valuable baseball card in the world, a 1910 Honus Wagner card for which the pair paid nearly half a million dollars. They were close, indeed, and Gretzky felt as much devotion to the man as to his team.

As a result, Gretzky quietly requested a trade as the deadline neared so that Los Angeles could get something for him rather than lose him in the summer to free agency. On February 27, 1996, the Kings acquiesced, sending him to the Blues for Craig Johnson, Patrice Tardif, Roman Vopat, a 1st-round draft choice in 1997 (Matt Zultek), and a 5th-round draft choice in 1996 (Peter Hogan).

The move to St. Louis made sense because that's where Brett Hull was still playing, and the thought of having Gretzky as set-up man and Hull as sniper had everyone in the city drooling. Too, the coach was Mike Keenan who knew and admired Gretzky up close from the Canada Cup. When Gretzky arrived in St. Louis, Shayne Corson immediately handed his captaincy over to number 99.

Off ice, Gretzky's agent, Mike Barnett, was negotiating a three-year contract with the Blues to avoid free agency and to ensure Gretzky would end his career in St. Louis. All that changed literally overnight during the playoffs. The Blues defeated Toronto in six games in the first round, an expected result given the reverence Gretzky had for Maple Leaf Gardens.

In the second round, though, against Detroit, things took a serious turn for the worse. Detroit eked out a 3-2 win in the opening game of the series but blew the Blues away 8-3 in Game 2. Keenan publicly criticized Gretzky for his performance in that game and later that night, Jack Quinn, St. Louis president, took the contract offer off the table. "If that's all the faith they had in me—to take a deal off the table after one bad game—right then I decided I would never sign with the Blues, which I had every intention of doing," Gretzky said later.

St. Louis lost that series in double overtime of Game 7 thanks to a great goal by Steve Yzerman, and in the summer Gretzky decided to go to Broadway to close out his career with another friend, Mark Messier.

In all, Gretzky had 21 points in those 18 regular-season games with the Blues and 16 more points in 13 playoff games, a small segue on the road to the Hall of Fame.

Jaromir Jagr

Before the Pittsburgh Penguins selected Jaromir Jagr fifth overall at the 1990 Entry Draft, the star had been well known to any hockey lover. Jagr began playing for Kladno in the junior league in Czechoslovakia at the age of 12, and after four years he moved up to play for his hometown's senior team for two years. Earlier in 1990, the 18-year-old Jagr played at both the World Junior Championship in Finland and then in the spring at the senior World Championship. In the former he counted 18 points in just seven games as the Czechs earned a bronze medal. In the latter, in Switzerland, the Czechs won bronze again.

As soon as he was drafted, Jagr was destined for Pittsburgh, though not directly. He left Czechoslovakia and his team without authorization, a terrifying act for a teenager with family left behind. When he got to training camp that fall, he took the number 68 to remind himself daily of the Soviet tanks rolling through Wenceslas Square in the summer of 1968.

On the hockey front, he was surrounded by a team that could seriously challenge for the Stanley Cup, thanks most importantly to the presence of Mario Lemieux. Lemieux was in his prime, the clear heir to the throne of Wayne Gretzky, and over the years general manager Craig Patrick had assembled a fine group of players to help shoulder the load. Goalie Tom Barrasso had developed into a fine starting goalie; Paul Coffey was an anchor on the blueline; Mark Recchi and Kevin Stevens were offensive players who could score with or without Mario on their line.

Jagr was another piece of the puzzle. He was a rookie and only 18 years old, but he had already played serious hockey for two years. He arrived speaking almost no English, but on ice he was already big and exceptionally strong. His mullet and good looks made him a fan favourite, even if he couldn't say more than a few words that anyone could understand.

Yet everyone understood the language of hockey, and that was Jagr's first language, his language of choice. He played much differently than Lemieux, but still people wanted to compare the two. Because of his strength, he needed less time to adjust to the smaller rinks in North America than most players of his generation. So, coach Bob Johnson happily gave him more ice time more quickly than he might the average rookie.

Patrick's best move of this 1990-91 season came when he acquired Jiri Hrdina in December. Another Czech, he was brought in only in part because of his skill. He was also meant to be a companion for Jagr, lonely in a foreign land. Jagr played even better in response to having a Czech friend around. By the end of the season, he had 27 goals and 57 points, but it was clear these were small numbers compared to what he was going to record down the line as a mature player.

Jagr didn't win the Calder Trophy in 1990-91. That honour went to goalie Ed Belfour of Chicago. The runner-up was Detroit's Sergei Fedorov who had a similar relationship to Steve Yzerman as Jagr had to Lemieux in Pittsburgh. It was Jagr who ended the season the most satisfied, however, because the Penguins steamrolled their way to their first ever Stanley Cup. Lemieux led the team to an easy 8-0 victory in game six against the Minnesota North Stars, and there was Jagr, now 19, drinking champagne out of the Cup and hugging his idol, Mario. Few rookies before or since have had such an introduction to the NHL.

Joe
Sakic

Nobody feels more fortunate for being in the NHL than Joe Sakic. He was a very talented teen playing provincial junior hockey in Burnaby, British Columbia, before moving to Swift Current to play in the WHL in 1986 at the age of 17. As a rookie, he averaged nearly two points a game in a year marred by horror. The Broncos were on a bus trip between games when the bus skidded off the road. Four members of the team, teenagers, were killed. It was an accident that wrenched the small city but brought the players and citizens closer at the same time. From that day on, Sakic was happy to be alive, happy to have every day of family and hockey that his four friends would never have again. At season's end, he was blessed with good fortune—well earned—when Quebec selected him 15th overall at the draft.

He returned to Swift Current the next year and had a season worthy of the record books. He scored 78 goals and 160 points, both tops in the WHL, in a mere 64 games. He was named WHL and CHL player of the year, and did so in style. Midway through the season he played for Canada at the World Junior Championship, helping the team win gold. "It pains me to say it," his coach said at the end of the year, "but I think Joe has passed junior hockey by. I don't expect I'll be getting him back net year." Those words came from Graham James, the Broncos' coach and the man who was jailed years later for sexually abusing Sheldon Kennedy. That Sakic and his teammates could function at all under such a man seems, in retrospect, a miracle.

Sakic is not the biggest player or the toughest, but he may be the most complete and he is surely the quietest of the great stars of the ice. His game is defined by his extraordinary wrist shot and his ability to see the whole ice at all times. He scored 23 goals as a rookie with the Nordiques, the worst team in the league, and he displayed superior passing and a physical ability at 19 to play with the big boys. Every year he got better, and every year the team improved as well. In just his second season he reached the 100-point mark, but it wasn't until his fifth year that the team finally made the playoffs.

In 1992, Sakic was made team captain and three years later the Nordiques relocated from beautiful Quebec City to Denver, Colorado. By that time, the Avalanche was a Cup-quality team, and in the 1996 playoffs the Avs reached their greatest heights. During the regular season, Sakic scored a personal-best 51 goals and 120 points, third best in the league. In the playoffs, he proved his worth by scoring six game-winning goals, an NHL record (since eclipsed by Brad Richards (seven) in 2004). Two of those winners came in overtime. In all, Sakic had 18 goals in the playoffs, second-most in NHL history. He recorded four assists in a Cup finals game to tie a league record and had a hat trick in the opening round against Vancouver. Sakic was awarded the Conn Smythe Trophy for his dominance, and after the final game of the four-game sweep of Florida, he got to hold the Cup high above his head, his childhood dream finally realized.

Five years later, in the spring of 2001, he again won the Cup during perhaps his best career year. He had 118 points in a league that was vastly more defensive than when he had 120 points, and he won both the Hart and Pearson Trophies for his outstanding season. Yet after being given the Cup on ice by NHL Commissioner Gary Bettman at the final horn, Sakic did not lift it high above his head as was tradition. Instead, he swung it to his right and allowed teammate Ray Bourque that honour, a gesture that defined the classy Sakic as much as any single goal or assist he ever recorded.

Maurice "Lefty" Reid

Before players took the Stanley Cup home for a day in the summer, before the white gloves of Phil Pritchard and Craig Campbell as they brought the trophy out for presentation after the final game, before the Hockey Hall of Fame moved into its swank new digs in downtown Toronto, there was "Lefty" Reid, the curator of the Hall, keeper of the Cup, and custodian of world hockey history.

Reid became curator of the Hall in February 1968 upon the retirement of Bobby Hewitson who had been the man in charge since the Hall opened its doors at the C.N.E. in 1961. Reid set about to take the Hall to a new level of sophistication and put it on par not with other hockey collections but with other national museums. He saw the Hall as a cultural institution, a repository for everything to do with the history of the game, past and present, local and international, amateur and professional.

It was Reid who spent his first summer on the job updating and re-writing player biographies, notably the lives of the game's early great players. This project dovetailed with his other first ambition which was to create, develop, and maintain a hockey library that would define that history of the game. He cut out newspaper clippings on everything related to the game; he hunted down photographs and photo collections; he acquired books, one at a time, to build an archive second to none.

Reid was Stanley Cup custodian long before the term ever really existed. The Cup was in his daily care at the Hall, of course, but for 17 years it was also his responsibility to take the great trophy to the arena where it would be won every spring. Upon retiring, he revealed that the thing that made him happiest (and, no doubt, most relieved as well!) was that during his time with the Cup nothing bad ever befell the great trophy!

If not for "Lefty" Reid, the historic Turofsky Collection might have ended up in hands outside Canada which would have been a terrible loss for the mother country of the game. If not for him, the Hall would not have in its possession, as it does today, at least one photo of virtually every NHL skater. If not for him, the international section of the Hall would have had much poorer representation of the early years. If not for him, Jacques Plante's incomparable collection of masks would surely have been sold piecemeal elsewhere around the world.

Reid encouraged visits to the Hall by teams and players from around the world to showcase the work he was doing and explain firsthand how essential it was that hockey had a living, breathing museum which it could call its own. He created exhibits based on his acquisitions and acquired other pieces by creating new exhibits based on his needs. Twice, Reid organized a traveling display of the Hall's collection and took it on the road for extended periods. In 1971, he took an exhibition to Calgary, and eight years later he went on an ambitious, ten-city tour of the United States.

Before Reid, of course, many great hockey historians saw the value of the game's stories and artifacts, but in "Lefty" the Hockey Hall of Fame had its first true curator who actively tried to enrich the museum (a term he officially added to the name) through acquisitions and donations. Every day he worked, he was on the phone asking NHL teams for sweaters, retired players for artifacts, collectors for memorabilia to add to the Hall, either for display or preservation and posterity. How appropriate, then, that it was "Lefty" who was the first official Hall employee to carry the Stanley Cup out to the NHL president and the victorious NHL captain every spring year after year.

Martin Brodeur

Patrick Roy has barely retired but already his amazing records might well be in jeopardy if Martin Brodeur keeps playing as he has. And why wouldn't he keep going? Since becoming New Jersey's starting goalie during the 1993-94 season, he has been the very paradigm of consistency and high-level of play.

Brodeur was drafted by the then-lowly Devils in 1990 midway through his junior career with St. Hyacinthe in the QMJHL. He got his first NHL start under emergency circumstances. On March 26, 1992, he was called up from St. Hyacinthe after both Chris Terreri and Craig Billington were unable to play. He allowed just two goals in a 4-2 win at home. Brodeur played just four regular season games and two more in the playoffs that year, but it was clear he had something special. The next year, he was in Utica from start to finish, developing with the team's farm club.

He began his NHL career in 1993-94 when Peter Sidorkiewicz was injured and Brodeur was Terreri's backup to start the season. Every time he played, however, he was sensational, and soon the positions were reversed such that Brodeur was the starter and Terreri the backup. In the playoffs, he guided the team to game seven of the Conference finals before losing to eventual Cup champions Rangers. Nonetheless, Brodeur won the Calder Trophy and the year after he came to training camp as the man to beat in the New Jersey crease.

It was a lockout-shortened season, but Brodeur played 40 of 48 games for the team and in the playoffs of '94-'95 he was nothing short of brilliant. He won 16 of 20 games, that magical number attainable, of course, only by one goalie every year—the Cup winner. Brodeur and the Devils beat an up-and-coming Detroit team in four straight games, and just as Roy had been anointed St. Patrick after his performance at the 1986 finals for the Canadiens, so, too, Brodeur reached mythical status after an improbable New Jersey Cup win.

On paper, Brodeur's career seems almost boringly brilliant. He is known for his remarkable endurance, playing 70 games a year almost without exception for a decade. He is the only goalie in NHL history to win 30 games or more for ten years running. He won his 400th game in the fewest games (735) and at the youngest age (31 years, 322 days) than anyone in league history. He reached 75 shutouts faster than anyone, with one exception—Terry Sawchuk, the man who holds the all-time record of 103 shutouts, long thought to be one of the golden records of the game and never to be equaled. Brodeur has won the William Jennings Trophy for fewest goals allowed four times and the Vezina Trophy as best goalie twice. Most important, he has won big games all his life. After 1995, he won the Cup again in 2000 and a third time in 2003. He led Canada to gold at the 2002 Olympics in Salt Lake and to the World Cup of Hockey championship in September 2004.

In games, Brodeur is regarded as the best puckhandler among goalies. He is called the third defenceman and has 23 assists to his credit as a result of his ability to pass the puck to teammates quickly. Additionally, he is one of only two goalies (along with Ron Hextall) to score a goal in both the regular season and playoffs by actually shooting the puck the length of the ice into the empty net.

Mike Modano

The NHL's Entry Draft is something of a crap shoot. In some cases, it's easy to see when an 18-year-old is on the verge of becoming a superstar (Mario Lemieux), but in other cases that teenager's ability proves to be a red herring in determining his abilities over a 15-year career. In 1988, Mike Modano was selected first overall, by Minnesota, but some of the other players selected in that first round proved how difficult drafting can be by not living up to their potential as Modano has done.

The Stars were torn between Modano and Trevor Linden. Both were excellent offensive talents. Modano was deemed faster with the better shot, but he was notorious for shying away from the physical aspects of the game. Linden was not. Both played in junior leagues in Canada, so they were equally prepared for a long, NHL season.

Nearly twenty years on, Modano has accomplished more than Linden, perhaps, thanks to a Stanley Cup in 1999, but both players have left their mark on the game.

Not so for the fourth pick, Darrin Shannon, or the fifth, Daniel Dore, who was coveted by the Quebec Nordiques. Both had unimpressive careers, but further down the first round list were Rod Brind'Amour in ninth and Teemu Selanne in tenth who have also had fine careers.

Modano had a tough assignment with the Stars in 1988. The team wasn't very good, and the last American number-one selection was Brian Lawton who was a decided disappointment in the league. Still, Modano wisely chose to play one more year in the WHL with Prince Albert after being drafted—a year that included an injury and a second trip to the World Junior Championship—and when he made the Stars in 1989 he was a bigger and faster 19-year-old (although he made his NHL debut briefly in the 1989 playoffs).

As a centreman, he came to Minnesota and proved his worth as the number-one drafted player. He used his size well and established himself as a first-rate playmaker. By the end of his rookie season, he scored a very respectable 29 goals and had 46 assists as well. Indeed, his first three years were pretty much the same, but signs suggested that his skill outweighed his performance to date. His biggest fault seemed to be not his physical play but his desire, something he believed was connected with the team's overall poor performance. That changed at the end of his third season, though, when the team went to the Stanley Cup finals, only to lose to Mario Lemieux and Pittsburgh in six games.

In 1992-93, though, Modano had what was called a breakout season. He scored 33 goals, not spectacular, but added 60 assists for 93 points, ranking himself among the elite players. The team moved to Dallas the year after and with a newly-signed, multi-million-dollar contract in his pocket Modano was expected to deliver. He did. That '93-'94 season saw him reach 50 goals for the first (and only) time of his career.

Modano helped USA win the inaugural World Cup in the fall of 1996 and he went on to play at the three NHL Olympics, winning silver in 2002. In fact, he has played for his country at every step of his career, from the World Juniors to the 1991 Canada Cup, the World Championship in 1990, 1993, and 2005, and the Olympics.

His biggest day, though, came in the spring of 1999 when the Stars beat Buffalo to win the Stanley Cup, the apotheosis of a decade of NHL life. Amazingly, however, Modano has never won a major individual award. Nonetheless, he has played more than 1,000 games and reached the 1,000-point mark in 2002-03. He is almost certain to reach 500 goals before he retires. In all, Modano made the Minnesota scouting staff look smart, clearly a number-one selection who has had a number-one career. Not many top draft choices can boast as much.

Mike Richter

Mike Richter might not rank among the greatest goalies of all time, but he was a great goalie at the right time often enough that now that his career is over and his accomplishments counted, his was an exceptional career, to be sure.

On the night of February 4, 2004, his number 35 was hoisted into the rafters of Madison Square Garden to honour the goalie who spent his entire 15-year career with the New York Rangers, a fitting final chapter for a man who gave the city virtually all its hockey pride in that era.

By the time he was a full-time member of the Rangers, starting in 1989-90, Richter was already a veteran of the game at a high level. He had played in two World Junior Championships, two senior World Championships, and the 1988 Olympics.

He joined the Rangers at a time when they were a slowly-developing team on the upswing. As a rookie, he had a record of 12-5-5 behind starting netminder John Vanbiesbrouck. The following year, now sharing the duties with Vanbiesbrouck more or less equally, he was 21-13-7. In the fall of 1991, he was the starting goalie for USA at the Canada Cup, a tournament in which the Americans advanced to the finals for the first time before losing to Canada.

Strangely, Richter and the Rangers missed the playoffs in 1992-93, but starting the following fall the goalie was arguably the best in the business for a stretch of about three years. Of course, no one can deny Mark Messier his place in Manhattan's sporting history for his leadership and performance in the 1994 playoffs, but Richter was the backbone of that team's Stanley Cup run from start to finish. In the regular season he was almost unbeatable, compiling a record of 42-12-6 to go with a 2.57 GAA. In the playoffs, he was even more dominant, recording four shutouts in 23 games and allowing just two goals a game. The result was the Rangers' first Cup in more than half a century. Messier won the Conn Smythe Trophy, but Richter could have been given the award without a note of controversy.

The next great feather in his cap came in September 1996 when he almost single-handedly took USA to victory over Canada in the best-of-three finals of the World Cup. Richter was particularly impressive in the second period of game three when Canada outshot his team 22-9 but scored only once to tie the game. He foiled one great chance after another, and late in the third the Americans pulled away to a 5-2 victory. Richter was named tournament MVP uncontested.

In the modern game, Richter's career ended somewhat oddly. He suffered a concussion late in the 2001-02 season when he was hit in the head by a puck, and then early the next year, just days after posting his 300th career win, he was hit in the side of the head after turning away from a slapshot. The result was another concussion the symptoms of which never went away in the ensuing months. Wisely, Richter retired.

When all the wins and saves are tallied, Richter stands as one of the greatest American-born goalies of all time. He reached the 300-win club and played in three Olympics for his country. Most important, his legend lives largest in New York where he was such an important member of the city, in the blue ice for the Rangers and in the community for the people of the city he came to love and live with.

Pat Quinn

APRIL 28, 2001

Quinn

Having been in the coaching game for nearly three decades, Pat Quinn is thought of more as a man who stands behind the bench than one who used to sit on it as a player during NHL games. Indeed, the burly defenceman started his career with the Leafs in 1968 after playing several years in the depths of the minors. Two years later, he joined Vancouver, and in 1972 he was claimed by the new Atlanta Flames in the Expansion Draft. It was in Georgia that he spent the last five years of his playing career, a career that was cut short when he slipped on his son's skateboard in the driveway of his home and broke his leg so badly he had to retire.

Retire he did, but give up he did not. He almost immediately started coaching in the Philadelphia system, and midway through 1978-79 he became the team's head coach. A year later, he took the Flyers to the Cup finals where they lost to the Islanders in six games when Bob Nystrom scored in overtime. That first full season was historic for another reason. During the regular season, the Flyers posted an amazing 35-game unbeaten streak, to this day the longest in NHL history. The team finished with a mark of 48-12-20 but couldn't beat the Islanders who were on the way to their dynasty of four Stanley Cup victories in a row.

Quinn was fired just before the end of the '81-'82 season but after two years off he was hired by the Kings to coach in Los Angeles. He had earned his law degree from Widener University, Delaware School of Law in the interim, but the only bench that interested him was at the hockey rink. As in Philly, though, the team went from good to bad, and a strange controversy ended his days in Los Angeles nonetheless.

The Vancouver Canucks signed Quinn to an agreement in December 1986, while he was still coaching the Kings, for him to become GM and president of the team to start the next season. This was a violation of league rules, so NHL president John Ziegler expelled Quinn from the NHL until 1990 (nearly four years), and fined the Canucks a whopping $310,000 (which was later reduced in court to $10,000).

After the forced absence, Quinn, indeed, took over in Vancouver, and for most of the next five years he was in charge. His greatest success out west was another near miss with the Cup, this time in 1994 when the team went to game seven of the finals against the New York Rangers at Madison Square Garden.

Quinn was fired early in the '95-'96 season but was never far from the game. He was named assistant general manager to Canada's 1996 World Cup team, which lost to USA in the best-of-three finals, and the following spring he was assistant GM for Canada at the World Championship, which Canada won. Quinn reached the pinnacle of attention when the Leafs hired him to coach starting in 1998-99, and it was in Toronto that he lasted longest.

In seven seasons he reached the playoffs six times, thrice eclipsing the 100-point mark in the regular season for the first times in franchise history. He was also named head coach to Canada's entries at the three most important international tournaments in this era—the 2002 Olympics, 2004 World Cup, and 2006 Olympics. He was successful in the first two, but a dismal seventh-place showing in Torino in 2006 probably spelled the end of his international career.

Quinn is among the all-time leaders in games coached and victories, and now, in the twilight of his career, the man who started in the game as a bruising defenceman has left a legacy behind the bench that is among the finest in the game. All he needs is a Stanley Cup to make his life's work complete.

Peter Stastny

The many lives of Peter Stastny together form one of the greatest hockey careers the game has ever known.

First, there were the early international years with the old Czechoslovakian team. At 19, he played in the World Championship in 1976. Later that year, he played at the inaugural Canada Cup. He went on to play three more World Championships and the 1980 Olympics before ever setting foot in the NHL.

Stastny defected to Canada with his brother, Anton, soon after Lake Placid, and their other hockey-playing brother, Marian, came a year later. This made up part two of Peter's great career. The three brothers embraced the NHL, life in Quebec, and playing for the Nordiques. In seven of his first eight years Peter recorded 100 points or more. In fact, in the 1980s the only player to have more points than Peter Stastny was Wayne Gretzky.

Stastny caused a stir at the end of his first season when he won the Calder Trophy. A seasoned pro from Czechoslovakia, he was 27 by the time he came to the NHL and critics felt he was hardly a true rookie. The league later changed Calder Trophy regulations as a result.

In 1984, the political landscape was radically different from today. Once he left Czechoslovakia, there was no going back. As a result, he became a Canadian citizen and represented Team Canada at the 1984 Canada Cup. There was some indignation in Canada because he was taking a roster spot from a "true" Canadian, but facts were facts and he was eligible to play. Canada won that tournament with Stastny in the lineup.

Stastny went on to play for New Jersey and St. Louis toward the end of his NHL career, and during these years perestroika freed Iron Curtain countries from the vice-like grip of Communism ruled by the Soviet Union. One result was that the empires of the Czech Republic and Slovakia split. Stastny, embracing his independent motherland, played for Slovakia at the 1994 Olympics and later at the World Championships, helping the small nation become part of the A Pool family of great international hockey powers.

After retiring, he became general manager of the national team and experienced perhaps his most satisfying moment in 2002 when Slovakia won gold at the World Championship.

The final phase of his career started back in Quebec City during his early NHL days. He and his wife had a son, Yan. Yan was brought up in Quebec City, then spent his formative years in New Jersey and St. Louis where he developed into a fine young hockey player. Yan was drafted by Boston in 2002 and in 2005 he made his international debut at the World Championship—playing for USA! There, in the stands, was father Peter, a Hall of Famer, the greatest player ever to come out of Slovakia, a national hero in Bratislava, cheering for his son wearing the red, white, and blue of the United States!

Robert Reichel

For anyone who thinks the NHL and international hockey are the same, one needs to look no further than the life and times of Robert Reichel to think otherwise. Ask any NHL-wise person who Reichel was, and he'll say an average player with decent scoring ability who lacks that intensity to do much in the playoffs.

Ask a European who knows his international hockey and he'll say Reichel is one of the gods of Czech hockey, a long-standing captain of the team who has brought medal after glorious medal to the country. Go figure.

Reichel's NHL life is not easy to summarize. He was drafted by Calgary in 1989 and joined the Flames a year later at age 18. In his first two seasons he had 19 and 20 goals, but in years three and four he doubled that total to 40 each time. Yet in 13 playoff games in that stretch (two first-round losses), he scored just twice.

He wanted more money, played in Germany for half a year, came back and scored 18 times in 48 games. That summer of 1995, he lost his arbitration case with the Flames and in a fury went to play in Germany again for a year. He scored 47 goals in 46 games that season. He returned to the Flames a season later, but he wasn't the same player. He bounced around from team to team, ending his NHL career playing three years with the Leafs (2001-04). He never came close to winning the Stanley Cup, never won an individual award, and never played in an All-Star Game.

In Europe, during the same period, Reichel played in Germany for three years. He is a dual citizen of that country and Czech Republic and his brother, Martin, has played internationally for Germany for years. Robert also played for Litvinov for several years where he was revered.

Internationally, Reichel played in three World Junior Championships (1987-89) and nine senior World Championships in 1990, 1991, 1992, 1996, 1997, 1998, 2000, 2001, and 2003. As well, Reichel played in the 1991 Canada Cup, 1996 World Cup, and 1998 and 2002 Olympics.

Here's the amazing part. Reichel was captain of the 1998 team that won gold at Nagano. This was midway through a season with the New York Islanders which ended in the team missing the playoffs and permitting Reichel to return to the World Championships. At his first senior Worlds, in 1990, he won a bronze medal. In 1992, he won another bronze. In the years 1996-98, he won gold, bronze, bronze. In 2000 and 2001, he won two more gold, captaining those teams. At those early three World Junior tournaments, he won a silver and bronze medal.

Reichel was a European who simply didn't have the stamina or ambition to play NHL hockey in the NHL, spending year after year away from home and family. His forte was representing his country and playing the top level international tournaments. In that atmosphere, he was admired by all those Czech players who were so superior to him in the NHL. On the European stage, he was the player who led by example, and more often than not, he proved to be a winner. It's only in North America that nobody knows as much!

Roger Neilson

Hockey's Einstein, Roger Neilson was a complex man, a universal man, a man who meant everything to hockey and who owed his life to the game. He was never the best coach or the most successful, but he was beloved and respected by all. If ever a man were going to be buried at centre ice upon his demise, Neilson would have been the man. He was part of the piping, the paint, and the play.

As a kid, Roger Neilson played hockey like most Canadian boys. He was a goalie, good, to be sure, but not good enough to think about a career in the crease. Instead, he took to coaching, and in 1966, at age 32, he became boss of the Peterborough Petes in what was then called the OHA (today's OHL).

During his decade with the Petes he learned how to win but also how to challenge the system. He knew the rule book better than anyone and sometimes made a mockery of it, telling his goalie, for instance, to leave his stick lying across the goal crease in the final minute when he came to the bench for an extra attacker.

The Leafs hired him in 1976, and so began 26 years in the NHL with some ten teams as head coach or assistant. In 1999, he was diagnosed with multiple myeloma-bone marrow cancer, and after fighting this battle for 14 months he was given the worse news that malignant melanoma, a form of skin cancer, had also invaded his body.

He continued to coach whenever healthy, and at the end of the 2001-02 season the Ottawa Senators extended him an honour unlike any other. Neilson had been the team's assistant, but a fan noted that Roger's head coaching record stood at 998 games. Why not, the fan suggested, have head coach Jacques Martin "step down" for the final two games of the regular season so Roger could make it to an even 1,000?

Neilson was also inducted into the Hockey Hall of Fame in 2002, and was given the Order of Canada. It was a good year for a dying man.

Neilson never married and had no biological children, but his family numbered in the thousands. His hockey camp ran year after year, and it continues to use his name posthumously. He set up a hockey camp in Israel because he admired how people there wanted to play the game. He ran coaching clinics at which many of the great NHL coaches came to talk hockey and strategy. He was respected by absolutely everyone, and upon his death in June 2003 he was dubbed the most loved man in hockey. His funeral was a who's who of hockey people, players and coaches, NHLers and amateurs, active people and retired.

He coached so many teams it's difficult to picture him behind any one bench at any one time. Perhaps it was in Toronto where he was so loved by players and fans, but not by owner. Perhaps Vancouver where he waved a white towel in mock surrender during the 1982 playoffs. Perhaps in New York where he was close to winning the Cup, or Philadelphia where he was dismissed because of his illness. Or Ottawa, where it all ended. Neilson never seemed so affiliated with any one team so much as the game itself. His dry lips and furrowed brow and amiable disposition created a face that immediately said 'hockey.' And for that, everyone in the game should be humbled.

Steve Yzerman

When the 18-year-old Steve Yzerman made the Detroit Red Wings at his first training camp in the fall of 1983, he slipped quietly into the number 19 sweater vacated by Randy Ladouceur who remained with the team but switched to 29. Twenty years on, it is clear no one will ever wear 19 for Detroit again. Yzerman scored a goal in his first NHL game, against goalie Doug Soetaert of Winnipeg, and for more than two decades he has been the heart and soul of the Motor City. Yzerman saw the bad times—the worst times of all time, in fact—and then lived to tell of the great times—as great as any the city has experienced.

Along the way, Yzerman has gone from a sensational, speedy scorer to a savvy, two-way man. He has gone from an explosive offensive talent to a calm and mature leader. He has gone from trade rumour to Stanley Cup champion, and he has gone from energetic young pup to war-ravaged veteran.

At 18, Yzerman had no fear. He led the league as a rookie with 39 goals and 87 points, portents of greatness to come. His totals for year two were similar, but the following season was a shortened one because of a broken collar bone. In 1986, at the start of his fourth season and still just 21 years old, he became the youngest captain in team history. The Wings, which had fared poorly in his three previous years in the playoffs, rallied behind their young star and went to the Conference finals before bowing out.

Yzerman then embarked on a streak of six successive years with at least 100 points, scoring 50 or more goals five times in that stretch. Yet the team's chase for the Cup ended abruptly every year. By this time, the now veteran superstar was being questioned for his ability to take the team to the finals and rumours of his being traded were as common as his goals and assists.

Of course, Yzerman survived those rumours. He reiterated his love for the city and his desire never to play elsewhere, and the team got better. Scotty Bowman came in as coach, and Bowman brought in a group of Russians to form a five man unit that was the talk of the league. No longer the sole and all-encompassing focus, Yzerman became a better all-'round player and the team started to win more when it counted the most—in the playoffs.

In 1995, the team broke through, advancing to the finals before being swept aside by New Jersey in four games. It was tantalizingly close, but not good enough. The next year they lost to Colorado in the semi-finals, but the year after they won the first Cup for Detroit since 1955. The year after, they won again, Yzerman being named Conn Smythe Trophy winner for his superb playoffs. By this point, he settled into becoming a player who could both score and play responsibly in his own end. No one in the league was scoring 60 goals and 150 points any more, and if he were to prolong his career, he needed to work on play inside his own blueline. Unselfish and responsible, he did just that.

The team won another Cup in 2002, a year in which he also won a gold medal with Canada at the 2002 Olympics. In capturing both honours, Yzerman was hailed for doing so on virtually one good knee. Right after the Cup triumph he underwent serious surgery to reconstruct one of his knees, a career-threatening procedure in light of the severity of the damage to the joint.

Amazingly, but not surprisingly, he recovered, and when he signed on with the Wings for 2005-06 at the age of 40, he was extending to 22 years his tenure with the club and to 19 his captaincy, the latter the longest tenure in NHL history.

Wendel Clark

The one and only time the Toronto Maple Leafs owned the first overall pick at the Entry Draft was back in 1985 when the team selected Wendel Clark. He had been a defenceman with the Saskatoon Blades in the WHL where he earned the reputation as the hardest-hitting player in that league. When he got to Toronto, though, his first priority was to save an ailing team from disappearance.

Clark skated his way into the hearts of Leafs fans from the moment he arrived in the city. He had an exceptional wrist shot, could hit with his shoulder that was pound-for-pound the heaviest hit in the league, and could fight for the welfare of his teammates as well. With Clark in the lineup the message was clear—we might not win every game, but in the ones we lose you're going to feel the pain as well.

The Leafs were such a bad team in 1985 that they needed Clark in the lineup that fall, a raw 18-year-old to inject some life into the moribund lineup. Clark didn't disappoint, but over time he paid the price. In his rookie season he scored an amazing 34 goals and had a weirdly disproportionate eleven assists. He racked up 227 penalty minutes, fighting any and every opponent who challenged him in order to prove his worth and his team's toughness. The Leafs made it into the playoffs that year for the first time in three years, and the Wendel Clark era was off to a smashing start.

Year two was impressive because Clark kept scoring (37 goals) and fighting (271 penalty minutes) and because he played 80 games. It was to be the only time in his career he played a full season. The year after, for instance, he played just 28 games because of a variety of injuries, notably to his back which was having a tough time enduring the rigours of his physical style of play. The year after, he appeared in only 15 games, and the year after that just 38. In those three years, Clark saw action in just 81 of a possible 240 games.

Nevertheless, Clark's popularity in the city soared and slowly but surely the team around him improved. He was named captain in 1991, a natural move after Rob Ramage left the team. These were the years that the Leafs brought Cliff Fletcher on board as general manager and Pat Burns as coach, acquired Doug Gilmour and Grant Fuhr via trades and became a top team very quickly. Clark now had a supporting cast to be proud of, and the team reached its peak in 1993 and 1994 when it reached the Conference finals both years.

That '93-'94 season marked the end of the Clark era. He scored 46 goals and was at the top of his game, but Fletcher decided to trade away his captain and star to Quebec in a deal that saw the Leafs acquire young Swede Mats Sundin.

Clark's only year in Quebec was marred by a serious head injury suffered when he slid heavily into the end boards, threatening his career. He recovered and was traded to the Islanders, all the while Toronto fans clamouring for his return. This happened at the March trade deadline in 1996, but his next year was tinged with disappointment. Although he returned to form by playing 65 games and scoring 30 goals, the team missed the playoffs. Clark was on the move the following year at the deadline, but after brief stints with Tampa Bay, Detroit, and Chicago he returned to Toronto for one last gasp, becoming the only player in team history to play for the Leafs on three separate occasions.

Clark's last great moment came during the 2000 playoffs when he finished an end-to-end rush by hitting the post with a patented wrist shot against Martin Brodeur and New Jersey. The Leafs lost the game and series, and Clark retired, a fan favourite, a great hitter, and a man who gave every morsel of his body to the game and, more specifically, to the Leafs.

Brent Sutter

Of course, all Sutters being cut from the same cloth, it is easy to blend the various family members into an indistinguishable polyester when in fact each was its own high-end suede. Amazingly, Brent was one of only two Sutters to win the Stanley Cup. He played on two Islanders' teams in the 1980s dynasty while brother Duane played on all four Cups on Long Island. Duane, who got to the Islanders first, was nicknamed Dog, so Brent was given the follow-up moniker of Pup.

More tellingly, Brent was one of only four players to win the three Canada Cups of his era—1984, 1987, and 1991 (the others were guys named Gretzky, Messier, and Coffey). That first in '84 was unique to him. He made the team only because his Islanders teammate Bryan Trottier decided to play for USA at the tournament. Brent then went on to have his best statistical year, scoring 42 goals and 102 total points.

His reputation was two-fold. Some say he was a goal scorer who could check; others called him the best checker in the league who could also put the puck in the net. Either way, he was deemed a star inside either blueline, and few players ever earned that sort of credit. It was this reputation which got him a spot with Team Canada time and again. He didn't have the skill of Gretzky or Messier, but he was the team's best faceoff man, an aggressive forechecker, hard-working backchecker, and utterly tenacious on the puck carrier.

It was only natural that Brent eventually became team captain with the Islanders, in the fall of 1987, the start of his eighth season. After four and a half years, he was traded to Chicago early in the '91-'92 season, and right away he helped the team reach the Cup finals before losing to Mario Lemieux and the Pittsburgh Penguins.

Brent retired in 1998, but like all Sutter brothers he remained very much in the game. He became coach and GM of the Red Deer Rebels, but only by happenstance. Immediately after hanging up the proverbial blades, he bought a ranch outside Red Deer to work with his wife and children. Then, Rebels' coach Terry Simpson asked him to drop by occasionally to coach the kids at practice every now and then.

Sutter ended up buying the team in May 1999 and decided to take on the dual roles of GM and coach. In his second year, the team won the Memorial Cup. In the summer of 2004, he was named coach of Canada's national junior team and at the 2005 World Junior Championship he led the team to victory in what many considered the best ever performance at that tournament. Canada was a perfect 6-0-0, scored 41 goals and allowed just seven. The team never trailed for one minute of the tournament.

The only other team that might be considered better was the 2006 Canadian team also coached by Sutter. The previous year he had a room full of 19-year-old veterans. In 2006, returning as national coach, he had just one player from the previous year. Yet Canada went 6-0-0 again and allowed only six goals all tournament, a record. Brent Sutter the player has become Brent Sutter the world-class coach seamlessly, one might say effortlessly. Except everyone knows the words Sutter and effortless never go in the same sentence. Never.

Canada Cup 1987

The last days of truly great international hockey, the 1987 Canada Cup remains a touchstone in Canadian history, second in importance only to the 1972 Summit Series. This tournament resonated on a personal and professional level, the former in the context of the friendship between Wayne Gretzky and Mario Lemieux, the latter because of the three-game, 6-5 finals series between Canada and the Soviet Union.

It was during Canada's training camp that Gretzky, the most dominant player of the 1980s, blasted his heir apparent, Lemieux, for lack of effort. Mario was undoubtedly as gifted a player as ever put on a pair of skates, but he didn't work for his skills in the same way Gretzky did. One practise, Gretzky tore into Lemieux, telling him to raise his level far above the one at which he was contentedly playing. Lemieux got the message and delivered a magical performance in the tournament, scoring eleven goals. Nine of those were assisted by Gretzky.

The round robin start to that year's Canada Cup wasn't pressure-filled because the top four teams advanced to the semi-finals, only the bottom two teams being eliminated. Nonetheless, both eventual finalists started off slowly. Canada settled for a 4-4 tie with Czechoslovakia on the first day in a game in which the Canadians squandered leads of 1-0, 3-2, and 4-3. The next night, the Swedes stunned CCCP by a 5-3 score.

Both teams then got on track to win their next three games to set up a game between each other. It was a round-robin game, and since both teams had established a good position in the standings it wasn't really do-or-die for either side. Still, the way each team played might dictate how the finals might be played. The result was a 3-3 tie. Canada scored the only goal of the first period, but the Soviets stormed back with three goals early in the second. Canada got one back before the end of that period, and then Gretzky tied the game at 17:33 of the third. This set up Canada-Czech and Soviet-Sweden semi-finals games. To no one's surprise, the two superpowers prevailed to set up a best-of-three for the ages.

In game one, Mike Gartner scored early but the Soviets took control and scored four in a row. Trailing 4-2 entering the third, it was Canada that rallied late, scoring three in a row to take a 5-4 lead with under three minutes to go. However, just seconds after Gretzky scored the go-ahead goal, Andrei Khomutov scored for the Soviets to send the game into overtime. Surprisingly, in the fourth period, the Soviets dominated, and Alexander Semak scored at 5:33 to give his team an impressive 6-5 win to take control of the series.

In game two, the momentum went back and forth. Canada again opened the scoring and led 3-1 after the first; the Soviets tied the game in the second; and, Lemieux put Canada ahead 4-3 before the second intermission. Valeri Kamensky scored at 18:56 of the third to tie the game 5-5 again, and another overtime had to be played. It wasn't until midway through the second extra period that Lemieux banged home a Gretzky shot to give Canada the win. It was Gretzky's fifth assist of the game. He estimated he played close to 60 minutes that night and later called it the best international game of his career.

This set the stage for game three, and although it didn't go to overtime, it felt like overtime when Lemieux buried Gretzky's pass with a bullet wrist shot over the glove of Sergei Mylnikov in the Soviet net at 18:34 of the third to make it 6-5 again (appropriately, the same score as game eight of the Summit Series). It was a dramatic and fitting end to a great series, and the Gretzky-Lemieux combination was perhaps the greatest dual performance in hockey history, certainly in Canada.

Canada's World Juniors 1991

Saskatoon was the host city for the 1991 World Junior Championship, the third time Canada had hosted this evermore prestigious celebration of hockey for players under 20 years of age. It turned out to be a golden celebration, too, as Canada won gold on the final day of the round robin with a goal late in the third period against the Soviet Union. John Slaney was the hero.

The WJC is special in Canada because of the intense fan interest, but it is unique also within the scope of players' careers. The team is not made up of the top prospects or the most certain NHL stars of the future or the players with the best reputation or highest draft selection. It is based solely on merit of play as the tournament is about to happen and in the context of the team style as a whole.

As a result, for instance, this 1991 team did not include Adam Foote, Darryl Sydor, and Yanic Perreault, all of whom would go on to have fine NHL careers. It also did not include NHL players Owen Nolan (Quebec) and Keith Primeau (Detroit) because those NHL teams promised to release their young stars only if they were guaranteed a spot on the team. That was not how Team Canada worked, and the players were not extended invitations.

The players who did form this team, paradoxically, did not to a man go on to have exceptional NHL careers, either. Some teens peak at this age and decline as the competition becomes more severe (i.e., the NHL), and so players like Slaney or Mike Craig or Pierre Sevigny went on to have perfectly pedestrian pro careers. One player who did go on to NHL stardom was Kris Draper, who had the distinction of being the first player to score his first NHL and AHL goal before scoring his first goal in junior hockey!

The 1991 tournament was played under the old IIHF system of a simple round robin. Eight teams played seven games, one against each opponent, and the top three teams earned medals. Although this method rarely featured dramatic conclusions, 1991 was a happy exception. As was so often the case, the games boiled down to Canada and the Soviet Union. Each team was rolling along nicely, the Soviets a perfect 5-0-0 and Canada 4-0-1, their lone blemish a 4-4 tie with USA in their second game.

On January 3, the second last day of the event, the Soviets played Finland, and a win would place them in the driver's seat heading to a last-day showdown against Canada. All seemed well with the Soviets leading that game 5-4 and time winding down, but then they got a late penalty and on the ensuing power play Jarkko Varvio scored at 19:45 to tie the game. This meant the final game would produce the gold medal, but there was one small problem for Canada. A tie in that game would mean a tie in the standings, and the first tie-breaking determinant was goals differential, which favoured the Soviets. In other words, the Soviets needed only a tie to win gold; Canada needed a win.

Canada started the game with the urgency that the situation required, building a 2-0 lead after 20 minutes thanks to goals from Sevigny and captain Steve Rice. The Soviets got one back in the second, though, and tied the game early in the third. They were now in control. Slaney, however, proved the hero at 14:47 when he beat Sergei Sviagin to give Canada a lead. He jumped so high in celebration that he sprained his ankle and had to sit on the bench the rest of the tension-filled game. Canada preserved the lead, though, and sang *O Canada* after the final horn.

Bill Ranford

Hockey: Edmonton Oilers Bill Ranford #30 in action vs. Pitts. Pirates; Pitts., PA

The general rule of thumb is that a great hockey team must learn to win. In order to do this, it must lose first, grow and mature, and then blossom into a Cup-quality team. Much the same can be said for goaltenders. A great goalie usually starts as a backup, performs well on those rare occasions when he gets a start, and slowly but surely earns a starter's role on the team through patience and great play. Such was how Bill Ranford went from being backup in Boston to Cup champion in Edmonton—and back!

Ranford was still a teenager late in the 1985-86 season when the Bruins called him up to play a few games. But he played so well that midway through the next year, one in which he started as backup to Pat Riggin, the Bruins traded Riggin and anointed Ranford their number-one man. Ranford responded, but the next year he was part of a similar trade involving Edmonton. The Oilers had believed Andy Moog was the heir apparent to Grant Fuhr, but Moog wanted a big contract and GM Glen Sather would not oblige. So, the Bruins and Oilers swapped goalies, and Ranford ended up back at square one, on a better team, but now backing up Grant Fuhr in Edmonton.

He persevered, though. In the 1988 playoffs, he sat at the end of the bench the whole time and watched Fuhr lead the Oilers to their fourth Stanley Cup in five years. The next regular season, Ranford slowly emerged as a capable goalie, and the year after he was number-one and Fuhr was on the bench (which eventually resulted in Sather trading Fuhr to Toronto).

The '89-'90 season saw Ranford prove his worth in spades. He had a regular season record of 24-16-9, and in the playoffs he was scintillating in leading the Oil to their most improbable Cup, one accomplished after Wayne Gretzky had been traded to Los Angeles. Ironically, the finals saw Ranford and the Oilers defeat Moog and the Bruins in five games. Ranford won the Conn Smythe Trophy for his performance that spring.

It might well be argued that up until the start of the 1994-95 season Ranford was the best goalie in the world. He followed his Cup win in the spring of 1990 by leading Canada to victory in the 1991 Canada Cup, a tournament in which he was clearly Canada's best player. From 1991 to 1994, he was the Oilers' best player and the main reason the team posted decent finishes in the standings with a sub-par team.

Ranford was also the main man in goal for Canada at the 1994 World Championship, a tournament Canada won for the first time since 1961 and which provided some small measure of atonement for the shootout loss to Sweden at the 1994 Olympics just weeks earlier. Appropriately, Canada won that World Championship gold in a shootout, 2-1, over Finland.

What goes up, must come down, and the following year Curtis Joseph was up and Ranford down. Ranford was traded back to Boston, and although he was the main man in goal the rest of the year, it was his last hurrah. He moved around four more times in the next three years, each team hoping he'd find his glorious touch in the crease, each team being disappointed and moving on. Ranford retired in 2000, long after his best days, but when all is said and done he can rightly lay claim to title of best goalie in the world for a good stretch of about five years. That's pretty exclusive company.

Bryan Trottier

The great New York Islanders' teams of the early 1980s featured the goal-scoring of Mike Bossy and the clutch goaltending of Billy Smith, and it is usually only after those two names does one call to mind the captain, Bryan Trottier. Yet without Trottier, make no mistake—Bossy wouldn't have scored as much and the Islanders wouldn't have won four straight Stanley Cups.

Trottier was the consummate professional. Driven to succeed, he was not the best at any one aspect of the game but by virtue of being probably second best at every aspect, he was in many ways the best overall player in the NHL during the height of his career. As a centreman, he felt it was his job first and foremost to get the puck onto the stick of linemate Bossy. As a result, Bossy eclipsed the 50-goal mark every season he played (excepting the last, injury-marred one) and Trottier invariably led the league in assists.

Trottier was perfectly capable of scoring, though. He scored at least 30 goals in each of his first nine years in the league (1975-84), culminating in '81-'82 when he hit the 50 mark for the first and only time. He also reached 100 points six times, leading the league with 134 in 1978-79. Most important, he elevated the play of his teammates through his own play, a quality few players can bring to a team. As he excelled, so, too, were those around him inspired to do same.

Trottier came to the Islanders by dint of a bit of a fluke. One of the team's scouts, Earl Ingarfield, went out to Swift Current where the 17-year-old was playing, merely to have a look at the team before he and some partners purchased it and moved it to Lethbridge. But team business took precedent over personal investment when Ingarfield saw Trottier play. The Islanders drafted the teenager that summer, and the rest, as they say, is history.

Despite his great career and contributions to the Islanders, Trottier was vilified by Canadians from coast to coast in the fall of 1984 when he decided to play for USA at the '84 Canada Cup rather than Canada, where he was born. He cited the fact that he had been living in the United States for a decade and married an American and produced American children, as reason enough to represent his adopted land. Back home, fans had none of it, and when he skated onto the ice in Canada to start the tournament, he was booed loud and long. To make matters worse, his presence helped the Americans to a 3-1-1 round-robin record, second only to the Soviets and superior to Canada's 2-2-1 record. It was only after Sweden demolished USA 9-2 in the semi-finals and Canada advanced to the finals with a dramatic 3-2 win (thanks to Bossy), that fans eased their criticism.

Once his usefulness had been used by the Islanders, they sent him to Pittsburgh where the now aging star helped Mario Lemieux and the Penguins win two Cups, in 1991 and 1992. Trottier spent the following year as an assistant coach back on Long Island, but when Lemieux missed much of the start of the following season with a bad back, Trottier came out of retirement and played a half a season more before calling it quits for good. By this time, he had some 1,425 points and six Stanley Cups to his credit, credentials aplenty to earn a spot in the Hockey Hall of Fame.

Dave Gagner

All Dave Gagner asked for was a chance, and whenever he got it, he played like he deserved it. He didn't always get it.

Gagner played his junior hockey with the Brantford Alexanders and did well enough on the scoresheet and in the dressing room to be drafted 12th overall by the Rangers in 1983. Rather than try to jump right into the Broadway lineup, Gagner spent the 1983-84 season playing mostly with the Canadian National Team in preparation for the Olympics in Sarajevo. The year went well for him. He played at the World Junior Championship in January '84 and then returned to the National Team for the Olympics the next month.

Gagner played most of that tournament on a line with Kirk Muller and Russ Courtnall, two other juniors, and although the team finished a disappointing fourth, the experience was worthwhile for Gagner, who scored a hat trick in an easy 8-1 win over Norway during the Games.

The next year, he turned pro with the Rangers, but life under GM Phil Esposito was anything but delightful for the rookie. Espo wanted more from Gagner sooner, expecting a high, first-round draft choice to become an instant NHL scorer. Gagner was not made that way and managed just six goals and as many assists in 38 games in his first year. He spent most of his first three seasons in the minors, but just before the start of the '87-'88 season he was traded to Minnesota.

He played 51 games with the Stars that year, and more in the minors again, but he never complained during his weeks with Kalamazoo and when he was called up he made the most of his time. The next year he made the team full time and delivered a consistently high level of play that Esposito had been wanting back in New York. Gagner scored 35 goals and 78 points and followed that with a 40-goal season the next year. Additionally, the Stars went all the way to the finals in '90-'91 (the Rangers lost in the opening round), and Gagner was among the top scorers, finishing with 27 points in the playoffs. It was the closest he ever came to the Cup.

Gagner continued to score for the next four years, recording seasons of 40, 31, 33, and 32 goals and establishing himself as one of the team's premier, and reliable, scorers. In 1993, the Stars out of the playoffs, he was invited to play for Canada at the World Championship, another feather in his hockey-playing cap. During the lockout of '94-'95, however, he lost his scoring touch, and when the season started up again he quite simply wasn't as effective. The last four years of his career (1995-1999) saw him dress for five different teams, but wherever he went he failed to bring his scoring stick with him. His best season during the twilight of his career came in Calgary in '96-'97 when he had 27 goals, but the team missed the playoffs.

Gagner retired in 1999 having scored 318 goals and 719 points, star totals, to be sure. More amazingly, though, was his ability to persevere during the dark days with the Rangers, remain confident in his abilities, and go to Minnesota with an open mind and healthy attitude. Winners don't quit, and Gagner proved himself a winner over a 946-game career.

New Jersey Devils 1990s

On November 19, 1983, the New Jersey Devils reached its nadir, losing to Edmonton 13-4 and having the ignominy of Wayne Gretzky calling the team a Mickey Mouse franchise. The Great One was right, but over the course of the next decade the team set about going from Mickey Mouse to penthouse, thanks in large part to Lou Lamoriello.

Lamoriello didn't come out of nowhere, but he made his mark on the Devils so quickly after being hired in 1987 that it may have seemed that way. He played college hockey for Providence in the early 1960s when U.S. college hockey meant precious little on the hockey map. From 1968 to 1983 he coached the Providence hockey team but was closely involved with baseball, basketball, and numerous other programs over the years. This led to his being named Athletic Director in 1983, a position he held for four years until taking the GM job offered by the floundering Devils.

Lamoriello brought a winning attitude to the front office, but more than that he brought tangible results. He drafted better. He made smart trades. He signed quality free agents. He brought respect to the dressing room and demanded professionalism from the athletes. In his first year with the Devils, the team went to the Conference finals. In 1990, he drafted Martin Brodeur. In 1991, he drafted Scott Niedermayer and acquired Scott Stevens as compensation for St. Louis signing Brendan Shanahan. In 1992, he traded for Bobby Holik. Slowly but surely, the superstar pieces fell into place.

Additionally, Lamoriello became famous for hiring coaches who would play a defensive system, boring to be sure, but successful even more sure. Larry Robinson and Pat Burns meshed with their GM to perfection, playing a trap system of defence that stifled even the most potent of offenses. Lamoriello also became famous for maintaining a strict budget and adhering to it even with his star players who often signed to play for less money than they could get elsewhere, knowing Cup victories were a fair price to pay for success.

In 1993-94, they made it to the Conference finals again, and the next year everything worked to perfection. The Devils swept Detroit in four straight games to win their first Stanley Cup. They were Mickey Mouse no more. Claude Lemieux was named Conn Smythe Trophy winner and Brodeur had a GAA of just 1.67 in the playoffs.

Under Lamoriello, however, the team proved this Cup success was not a one-off fluke. He signed Brodeur to a long-term contract because he knew success started in goal. Ditto for Stevens, a captain and leader and fierce hitter, and Niedermayer, the team's Bobby Orr-like offensive spark from the blueline.

Lamoriello also ensured veterans such as Ken Daneyko remained an integral part of the team while continuing to bring in fresh blood. Role players like Lemieux and John MacLean played alongside veterans such as Peter Stastny and Steve Thomas. They were replaced by Doug Gilmour and Dave Andreychuk while youngsters like Jason Arnott and Patrik Elias established themselves as the next generation of Devils' stars.

The Devils won a second Cup in 2000, went to the finals again the following spring, and won a third Cup in 2003. Their three championships in this time put them right beside Detroit for dynasty bragging rights, a level of success attributable first and foremost to the prowess of their GM, Lou Lamoriello.

Dominik Hasek

When Dominik Hasek was drafted a lowly 207th overall at the 1983 Entry Draft by Chicago, no one expected him ever to play in the NHL let alone play well enough for long enough to earn the moniker The Dominator.

Hasek was playing for Pardubice in Czechoslovakia, a Communist country that had no intention of allowing its best players to come to North America to play in an economy-based league like the NHL. And, in fact, it wasn't until seven years later that he did make his way to the Stadium in Chicago to begin his pro career.

When he did arrive, he found himself solidly on the bench as backup to Ed Belfour or playing down in the minors. Belfour was in the middle of a fine career with the Hawks, and after leading the team to the Cup finals in 1992, it was clear The Eagle was supposed to be their main man in goal for years to come.

By 1992, however, Hasek was a hero back home. Despite being only 25 years old, he had already played in five World Championships, two Canada Cups, and the 1988 Olympics, the best goalie in his native land. Such was Belfour's play, though, that the Hawks gave up on Hasek, trading him to Buffalo for Stephane Beauregard, another backup goalie, and a draft choice which turned out to be Eric Daze. In Buffalo, Hasek proved his worth beyond all doubt.

In just his second season with Buffalo, Hasek led the league with a GAA of 1.95 and played in a way that showed he could be the team's number-one man. He was, without doubt, the most unorthodox of the great goalies. He was not a butterfly goalie who went to his knees; he was not a standup goalie. Instead, he flopped and anticipated, gambled and sprawled and confounded shooters who didn't know what he was going to do or how he was going to play a shot. Hasek would play the shooter on a two-on-one, and if a pass came across the slot he fell on his back, splayed his arms, kicked up his legs, and turned his body in a contorted attempt to stop the quick one-timer from the back side. It looked utterly unconventional, but it was also consistently successful.

For several years the biggest problem was that Hasek was far and away the Sabres' best player. His maintained a stifling goals-against average around 2.00, but the team hardly scored more often and in the playoffs they routinely lost in the early rounds. Nonetheless, Hasek rose to his greatest heights in 1998 when the NHL participated in the Olympics for the first time. In the semi-finals, he confused all five Canadian shooters in a sudden-death shootout, and in the gold-medal game he shut out the Russians 1-0 to give the Czech Republic its first ever Olympic gold. Hundreds of thousands of fans greeted Hasek and the team in Wenceslas Square in downtown Prague after the victory, one of the greatest moments in Czech sporting history.

Back in Buffalo, the Sabres were putting together a quality team, and in 1999 they went to the Cup finals only to lose to Dallas on a controversial goal by Brett Hull in overtime of game six (Hull's skate was clearly in the crease). These were his greatest years. Hasek won the Lester Pearson Awards in 1996-97 and '97-'98 and was the first goalie ever to win consecutive Hart Trophies (in those same years). He realized his dream in 2001-02 when he took the Detroit Red Wings to a Stanley Cup victory to climax a career that had two parts to it: a sensational start in Europe, and a Hall of Fame finish in the NHL.

Doug Gilmour

93 GILMOUR

TOR-BUF

Photo: Paul BERESWILL

It was the biggest deal in NHL history, plain and simple. On January 2, 1992, Calgary and Toronto engineered a ten-player deal, all of them roster players, all starters. The Leafs sent Gary Leeman, Michel Petit, Jeff Reese, Craig Berube, and Alexander Godynyuk to the Flames. In return, they received Doug Gilmour, Jamie Macoun, Ric Nattress, Rick Wamsley, and Kent Manderville. The importance of the trade, to the Leafs, at any rate, far outstripped the names on the page.

First, this was the deal that established Cliff Fletcher as the Saviour of the Leafs. He had been hired by Donald Crump, who was put in charge of the Leafs after the death of Harold Ballard. Crump needed to hire a general manager, but knowing little about hockey he was smart enough to phone people around the league to solicit a variety of opinions. Fletcher was the name most people spoke the most highly of, and he was available and interested in the position.

Fletcher led the Flames to their only Stanley Cup, in 1989, and he knew the Calgary organization well. In fact, he hired Doug Risebrough as GM, and it was with Risebrough that the blockbuster deal was orchestrated. Risebrough was in a tough situation in Calgary because Gilmour had demanded a trade. His days in Calgary were numbered, as they say, and Fletcher took advantage of this knowledge.

The deal can be broken down into smaller sections, just as the two GMs no doubt did when they discussed its various parts. First, the goalies. The Leafs had Grant Fuhr, so Reese was a backup who could be traded without worry. Wamsley was playing behind Mike Vernon in Calgary, so this was a simple swap of backups.

Petit and Godynyuk were two defencemen, as were Nattress and Macoun. The difference was that the latter were the best tandem of defenders in the league for a number of years and were key to the team's Cup win in '89. They had played together since 1987. Petit and Godynyuk had been with the Leafs for about a year and were hardly the core of the blueline staff at Maple Leaf Gardens.

Berube and Manderville were the lesser forwards who swapped places. In Berube, the Flames got more toughness; in Manderville, the Leafs got more skill. In neither case, though, was the acquisition defining.

The centerpiece of the deal was Gilmour for Leeman. Leeman had scored 51 goals for the Leafs in '89-'90 but dipped to 17 goals a year later. Risebrough figured a new home might re-ignite the forward. Wrong. In truth, Leeman scored eleven goals over two partial seasons with the Flames before being dealt to Montreal. Gilmour, on the other hand, was a franchise player in Toronto. In his six seasons and 392 games, he scored 452 points and led the team to consecutive semi-finals appearances in the Cup playoffs, the best run the team had experienced in 15 years and more.

In 1992-93, "Dougie" set a franchise record with 95 assists and 127 total points. On February 13, 1993, he tied a team record by assisting on all six goals in a 6-1 win over Minnesota. In the '93 playoffs, he set another record with 25 assists and 35 points. A couple of years later, he scored his 1,000th career point while with the Leafs. By the time he was traded to New Jersey, he had established his place in the city's and team's lore as one of the greats. All thanks to the shrewd work of Cliff Fletcher and the assiduous work of Donald Crump first of all.

Doug Soetaert

Ask any player what the happiest day of his career was and most will say the day he was drafted. Ask others, more accomplished, and they will say winning the Stanley Cup. Soetaert can claim both milestones on his resume, and at the end of the day that's pretty good, indeed.

It was the Rangers who selected Soetaert at the 1975 Amateur Draft, but his first six years in the professional ranks were hardly what he had expected. During each and every one of those seasons he played only a handful of games in the NHL and spent most of his time in the minors. The lone exception was his last year, 1980-81, when he appeared 39 times for the Blueshirts. The trouble was that the Rangers had a number-one goalie in John Davidson, and it was only when Davidson was hurt, the '80-'81 season, that Soetaert had a chance at full-time duty.

Soetaert's big break came in the summer of 1981 when he was traded to the Winnipeg Jets. He played there for three years, and although he wasn't the number-one man, he was a very close second. In fact, for most of that time he split the crease duties with Ed Staniowski, outplaying Staniowski most of the time but falling short in playoff starts. Soetaert played 39, 44, and 47 games during those three regular seasons but only four of ten games in total in the playoffs. Those years were lean for the Jets because regardless what success they achieved over 80 games they were always eliminated in the playoffs by the Oilers. Always.

His big moment, not necessarily a break, came just before the 1984-85 season when he was traded to Montreal. Again, he was backup, but at least he was away from the Oilers. In 1985-86, Soetaert played 23 games during the regular season. In fact, on the night of February 23, 1985, he was pulled from the game against the Jets with the score tied 4-4 after two periods. He was replaced in the third by Patrick Roy, who was making his NHL debut, and the rest, as they say, is history.

The Habs won that game 6-4, and Roy took over as the number-one goalie for the rest of the year. Soetaert earned three shutouts during the regular season, but in the playoffs he didn't see a minute of action. Roy led the Canadiens to the Cup, though, and Soetaert got his name on the Cup as Roy's backup.

The next year, Soetaert was traded back to the Rangers where he played just 13 games. He had a poor record of 2-7-2 and a 5.16 GAA. Although his career came full circle and ended where it began, that start and finish were the least memorable moments. That was the end of the NHL line for him. After retiring, he became a coach for many years in the IHL until attaining executive status until the IHL folded in 2001. He then worked as a coach again with the expansion Everett Silvertips of the WHL for three years. In 2005, Soetaert became president of the Omaha Aksarben Knights of the AHL.

Grant Fuhr

By the time Grant Fuhr was inducted into the Hockey Hall of Fame in November 2003, his NHL debut was some 22 years in the past. In between, there was as much glory and fame as any NHL goalie had ever experienced in the game.

When the Edmonton Oilers spent a high draft choice in 1981 to claim Fuhr (8th overall), they were getting a player who was every bit as important to the team as any other of the Hall of Fame stars it would acquire. During the height of their powers in the 1980s, for instance, it was none other than Wayne Gretzky who said that if not for Fuhr the team never would have won as much as it did.

These were the years when Fuhr was deceptively great. After all, when the Oilers won a game 7-5, it was hardly the goalie who was going to be named the first star. Yet night after night it was his big saves that "preserved" that 7-5 win. In truth, Fuhr recorded exactly one shutout during his first six years of NHL play (255 games). This hardly speaks to greatness. Yet, during those first six years, the Oilers won the Stanley Cup three times. That is what mattered the most, and that is what history shows more approvingly.

During Fuhr's early years he was constantly fighting to be the number-one goalie with, most often, Andy Moog. Those first six years and three Stanley Cup championships, for instance, saw him start no more than 48 times a season, hardly an average figure for the starting goalie. Come the playoffs, however, it was usually Fuhr who started thanks to his reputation as the best money goalie in the world.

It wasn't until 1987-88, perhaps the best year of his career, that he established himself firmly as the one and only in the Oilers' crease. Fuhr started 75 of 80 games that year, won 40, and played 4,304 total minutes, all tops in the league that season. Again, more important, the Oilers won their fourth Cup in five years.

Just as Fuhr was coming into his prime, however, Bill Ranford arrived on the scene as an up-and-comer who had apprenticed under Fuhr and now seemed poised to take over. To make matters worse, just before the start of the 1990-91 season, Fuhr admitted to having a long-term problem with cocaine and was suspended the full season (a suspension that was later reduced to half a year). Ranford solidified his position, and Fuhr was traded to the Leafs at the start of '91-'92.

In some ways, 1995-96 was Fuhr's most impressive year in that he played 79 of 82 games, a modern-day record. He went on to win his 400th career game and retired in 2000 after a great career. In his prime, he was an active goalie in his crease, flopping from post to post, stopping breakaways occasioned by the all-too-frequent lapses by the goal-oriented Oilers. He is second all-time for goaltenders with 46 career assists, further testament to his ability to handle the puck and move it quickly to players heading up ice.

Fuhr never set records for individual achievement in the net. Dominik Hasek won the Vezina Trophy more often, Martin Brodeur had many more shutouts, and countless goalies had lower goals-against averages over the years. But Fuhr was a winner. He has his name on the Stanley Cup five times and he is among the all-time leaders in victories. That's why the Oilers lifted his number 31 to the rafters in October 2003, and that's why the Hockey Hall of Fame made him an Honoured Member a month after that. Greatness is sometimes measured by reputation and achievement more than statistics.

Guy Lafleur

A complex and idiosyncratic man off ice, Guy Lafleur was simple in his breathtaking ability on it. During the height of his powers, with the Montreal Canadiens in the 1970s, Lafleur won the Art Ross Trophy three years running (1975-78), produced six successive seasons of more than 50 goals and 100 points (1974-80), and played on five Stanley Cup teams.

Lafleur also wrote poetry, created a men's cologne called Number 10, recorded an album, opened a restaurant bearing his name, and gave up on his aspirations to become an RCMP officer so he could concentrate on hockey.

By the time he retired on November 26, 1984, at age 33, he was an Officer of the Order of Canada and a sure Hall of Famer. But in the first part of that last season in 1984-85, he managed only two goals and five points in the team's first 19 games. "I just wasn't motivated anymore," he explained the next day. "We had a good playoff last year and I was thinking about coming back and having a good year. But, as you know, I didn't score 20 goals in 20 games." More to the point, though, his coach, former teammate Jacques Lemaire, had cut Lafleur's ice time dramatically, and the proud Flower could not abide the indignity of sitting at the end of the bench.

That was not the end of that, however. In fact, even before being inducted into the Hockey Hall of Fame in September 1988, Lafleur discussed the possibility of playing with Wayne Gretzky in Los Angeles only days after 99 got married and was then traded to the Kings in the biggest deal in NHL history. "L.A. was my first phone call," Lafleur admitted on August 15, 1988. "It's a good place to play, especially now that Wayne is there."

The Kings didn't make him an offer, though. That was left to the New York Rangers who signed him on September 26, less than three weeks after his Hall of Fame honour. "Mentally, I'm ready," he declared. "Physically, I weigh six pounds less than I did the day I retired. I still think I can help a team for one or two years. Endurance will be the big thing, but I'm going to give it everything I've got, and for that I'll be proud of myself." Ironically, the Kings offered him a million-dollar contract the year after, but he turned that down to play for the Quebec Nordiques and finish his career in his home province.

The most anticipated game of his comeback was, of course, when the Rangers visited Montreal. That first game took place a week before Christmas 1988, but Lafleur missed playing in it because of a broken foot. Still, the Canadiens made a classy gesture by honouring him before the game. Guy limped out gingerly to centre ice to receive gifts from the team and a lengthy standing ovation from the sold-out crowd. His first game playing against his old team was delayed until February 4, 1989, and in that game Lafleur scored two goals, both of which shook the rafters with cheers from the Montreal fans who continued to love their Flower so much, even if he were wearing another team's sweater.

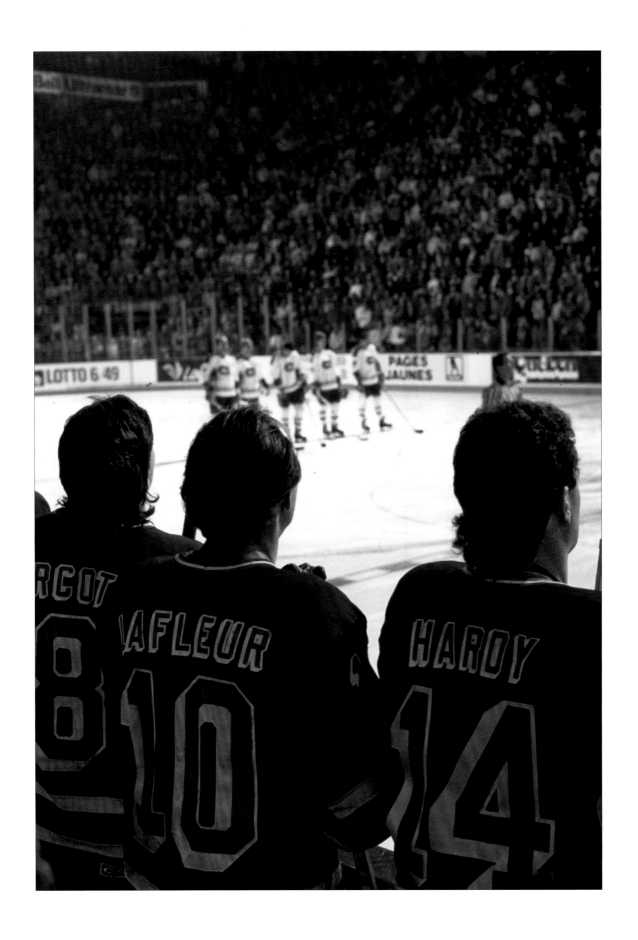

Jaromir Jagr

Hockey: Pitts. Penguins Jaromir Jagr #68 in action vs Montreal Canadiens; Pitts., PA.

The career of Jaromir Jagr can be neatly divided into three parts. The first is his initial foray into the NHL, the hotshot rookie and youngster who watched Mario Lemieux take their Pittsburgh Penguins to two Stanley Cup victories in 1991 and 1992. The second stage was with the same Penguins during the years of Lemieux's retirement when Jagr was the dominant player on the team (1997-2001). The third is his post-Pittsburgh career, first least successfully with Washington and more recently with the Rangers.

Even before Lemieux retired from the game at the end of the 1996-97 season, it was clear that Jagr was his heir. In his third and fourth seasons with the Pens, Jagr accumulated 94 and 99 points, respectively, and in the shortened '94-'95 season he won the Art Ross Trophy by virtue of having scored more goals than Eric Lindros, 32-29 (both were tied with 70 points). The next year, Jagr had his most impressive season, scoring 62 times and finishing with 149 points. In '96-'97, his last full season with Mario, Jagr finished with 95 points, but the team had a disappointing end to the year, losing in the first round of the playoffs to Philadelphia in just five games.

Jagr went on a tear without Lemieux in the lineup. He won the scoring race for the next four years, but despite his success the team's business viability was weakening. Lemieux became owner of the Pens and the economic realities of the game tempered the great number 66's ambitions. Lemieux knew he needed to build a new arena to keep the team in Pittsburgh, but until then he knew he had to trim the team's budget and improve the team's on-ice success, a paradoxical challenge if ever there was one.

During the transition from the Lemieux era to Jagr era in Pittsburgh, Jagr matured. He cut his mullet and became more tonsorially responsible. He stopped his saluting and double-fingered kissing after goals, and he assumed the team's captaincy. Further, he changed his attitude. There was no more pouting after a bad game, no histrionics, no looking at the referees for help. The one thing that never changed was his spectacular play, his strength in holding defenders at bay while he looked for a pass or got into position to shoot, his leadership through sheer numbers of goals and assists.

When Lemieux came out of retirement in December 2000, he did so in part because of his love for the game and in part because he needed the team to play better. Finances were such, however, that the Pens couldn't afford to keep Jagr on the team and pay him as he deserved. The result was a crushing trade. The best player in the game was sent to Washington with Frantisek Kucera for Kris Beech, Michal Sivek, Ross Lupaschuk, and future considerations. In short, the Pens lost a great player and got bit parts with small contracts in return. Devastated, Jagr had three uninspired seasons in the U.S. capitol and was traded to the Rangers in early 2003 straight up for Anson Carter.

All during his years in Pittsburgh, Jagr and Lemieux were far and away the stars, but after those two Cup wins the supporting cast with the Pens was lacking and the goaltending suspect. The closest the team ever came to another Cup was in Lemieux's first year back in the game, 2000-01, when Jagr had 121 points to lead the league and Mario chipped in with 76 points in just 43 games. They went to the Conference finals, but once there they were eliminated handily by New Jersey 4-1 in games.

Jagr's renaissance with the Rangers proved that he remains one of the great players of the modern game. And, with a consistent clampdown on obstruction, he has been able to work his magic in the opposition end with more success. Mario has now retired for good, and Jagr, now in his mid-thirties, has a little more time to try to win a third Stanley Cup before calling it quits himself.

Jeff Hackett

A well-regarded goalie in junior with Oshawa in the mid-1980s, Jeff Hackett had more bad luck than good during an NHL career that lasted exactly 500 games. Perhaps the bad luck started in junior. He was named to Canada's World Junior Championship team for 1988, and although that team won the gold medal, Hackett didn't see a minute of action.

In his three years with the New York Islanders, he played just a handful of games as a rookie, then all of his second year in the minors, and nearly half a season with the big club in 1990-91, compiling an unimpressive 5-18-1 record with a team that was not very good.

The Islanders lost Hackett to San Jose in the Expansion Draft of 1991. That first year he had a miserable record of 11-27-1 but was named the team MVP. Without his heroics, the team might not have even won those eleven games. The next year, however, Hackett was a dismal 2-30-1 with a lofty GAA of 5.28, a performance that sealed his fate in San Jose. He was traded to Chicago to act as backup to Ed Belfour, but now with a few years' NHL experience under his belt and playing on a better team, Hackett rose to the occasion. In fact, he rose so high he was often the better goaltender, much to the chagrin of Belfour.

Over his three years in the Windy City, Hackett played more and more games, won more and more frequently, and maintained a goals-against average just above 2.00. In fact, he finally won the battle of the goalies midway through '96-'97 because the Hawks traded Belfour to San Jose and made Hackett the clear starter. Just as things looked to get better, though, they got worse.

Despite having a great personal season in '97-'98, Hackett could not get the Hawks into the playoffs and as a result coach Craig Hartsburg was fired and replaced by Dirk Graham. The Hawks then got off to a terrible start the next season and Hackett was traded to Montreal. The Canadiens wanted him to be their starter while young Jose Theodore apprenticed under the veteran.

That trade started off wonderfully for Hackett. He had a 24-20-9 record with the Habs the remainder of the '98-'99 season, but the team missed the playoffs. The next year, the roles were reversed as the veteran Hackett acted as backup to the hot young Theodore. Hackett maintained this role for the better part of three seasons, but he never appeared in the playoffs for the Habs. Montreal traded him to San Jose, and the Sharks flipped him to Boston the same day, but Hackett was nothing but a spare part for a few weeks with the Bruins before becoming a free agent.

He signed with Philadelphia in the summer of 2003 in the hopes of re-establishing himself as a number-one goalie, but he suffered bouts of vertigo in Philadelphia that wouldn't go away. After a month of discomfort, he retired officially on February 9, 2004, after a career that had many upside moments that he couldn't maintain because of circumstance and, in the end, health.

Oddly, from the start of his career to finish, he played consistently well, but the team in front of him dictated to such a great extent the outcome of his own fortunes that some years it looked like he was a world-beater, other times a disaster. The truth is that under better circumstances he might well have turned into a true star goalie with staying power.

Jeremy Roenick

Love him or hate him, respect him or dismiss him, Jeremy Roenick is, if nothing else, very hard to ignore. From the first day he came into the NHL up to this very moment, he has been his own man and spoken his mind on every hockey subject under the sun. Along the way, he has racked up more than 1,100 points and earned a reputation as one of the finest U.S.-born players in NHL history.

The 1980s was, in many ways, the apotheosis of the modern game. It was a decade dominated by Wayne Gretzky and Mario Lemieux, two Canadians, but one in which the first wave of superstar Americans emerged and additionally the first wave of top-flight Europeans, from Peter Stastny to Jari Kurri, joined the league as well. Roenick came out of Thayer Academy, a Massachusetts high school, to play half a season in the QMJHL with the Hull Olympiques in 1988-89.

During that year, he was called up to Chicago on an emergency basis, but he played so well that the Hawks decided to keep him with the team. It was in part his contributions that got the team into the playoffs on the final weekend at the expense of Toronto, and in the playoffs he continued to impress.

Roenick was a fine skater, a pure scorer, and a tenacious centreman. The only thing he lacked at first was size and, at 19 years of age, physical maturity to play every night in the world's best league. In time, of course, he remedied these weaknesses. In his first full season he scored 26 goals and the Hawks went on to the Stanley Cup semi-finals before losing to eventual champions Edmonton in six games. Roenick had eleven goals in 20 games that post-season, and the year after he developed into the team's superstar, scoring 41 times and finishing with 94 points. In each of the next three seasons he topped the 100-point mark, but his scoring decreased after the lockout-shortened '94-'95 season when new coach Craig Hartsburg wanted his team to play more defensively.

Disgruntled, Roenick spoke out against his coach's mandate, but in so doing Roenick made no friends in the team's front office. He was eventually traded to Phoenix where he continued to score at least 30 goals, but there was often friction between him and the Coyotes management as well.

First, he refused to report to the team without a new contract to start the '96-'97 season, a declaration that had the added effect of costing him a place on Team USA for the inaugural World Cup. Despite his absence, USA defeated Canada in the best-of-three finals, and just a few days later Roenick signed the mega-deal he had been waiting for. Although he played up to his potential in the regular season, the team hardly fared well in the playoffs, and he, as one of the team's top players, was saddled with his share of the blame.

In the summer of 2001, Roenick signed as a free agent with the Flyers, but his time there was perpetually interrupted by injury. He suffered one well-photographed injury when an unpenalized high stick bloodied his lip badly, and on another occasion he suffered an horrific concussion (by his own count, the ninth of his career) after being hit flush in the jaw by a slapshot.

Along with Don Cherry and Brett Hull, Roenick is perhaps the most outspoken personality in hockey, venting during the year-long loss of NHL hockey, the state of the game, and whatever else comes into his head. Controversial and talented, Roenick has nevertheless given the NHL a more colourful palette with which to celebrate the self-proclaimed coolest game on ice.

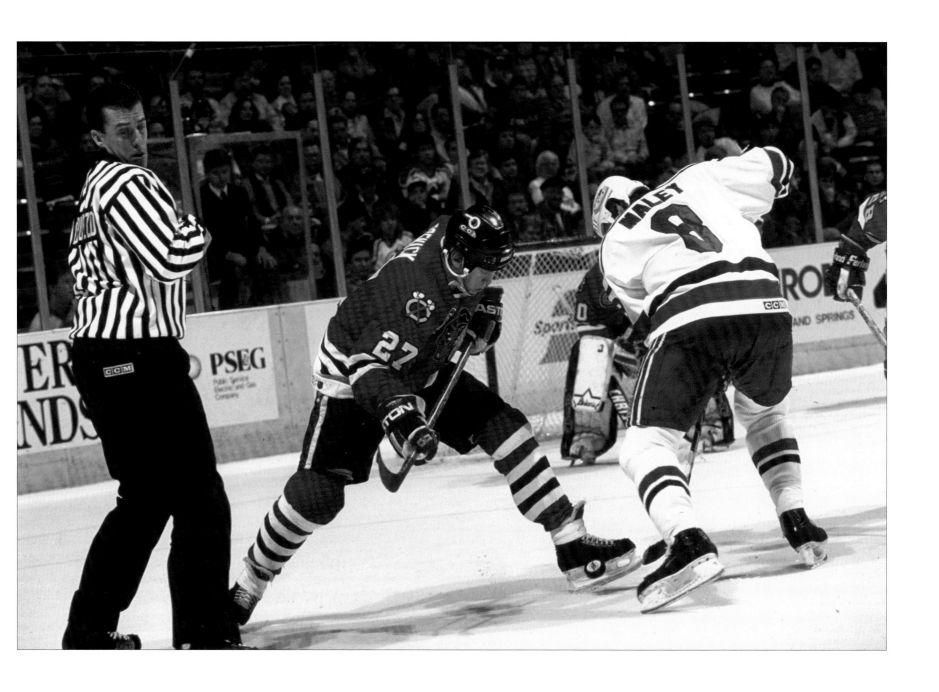

John D'Amico

With all the great players to have skated through the NHL over the years and decades, it isn't very often that an official leaves his mark in the way John D'Amico did by the time he retired in 1988 at the even age of 50. A professional, an amiable companion in a tough game, a fluid skater, D'Amico was everything the NHL could possibly ask an official to be.

He started his career in the 1964-65 season as a linesman, although he did work 22 games as a referee after expansion in 1967 when the league was in need of quality arbiters. He decided that he was more suited to working the lines, and it was in this capacity that he spent the rest of his career.

The life of a linesman is hardly easy. First, he is on the ice the entire game. Perhaps this doesn't sound like a big deal, but when D'Amico was in his last season, 49 years old, and a playoff game between the Islanders and Washington went to four overtimes, that represented a night's work that started at 7pm and ended at 2am. Non-stop skating with 15-minute breaks. Not many 25-year-olds could handle that assignment.

Then there is the game action. Again, a life that seems simple—stand at the blueline, call a few offsides and icings—was anything but. For instance, D'Amico once tried to break up a fight between Toronto's tiger Wendel Clark and St. Louis's big bruiser Charlie Bourgeois. The only person in that fight who got hurt was D'Amico himself who, in the process of disentanglement, took a punch over the eye that required stitches. A broken wrist, damaged knees, more cuts to the face, to thighs and arms, have all been part of his curriculum vitae during his NHL time.

Just like the players, D'Amico had to face all other players in the league, but his career lasted twice as long as most top players. He had to break up fights with Gordie Howe and Ted Lindsay, Dave Schultz and Tiger Williams, Dave Semenko and Marty McSorley. And, he had a schedule as tough as the players—same number of games, same travel, same hectic pace. Except, as a linesman, he had no home games!

On top of that, because he was the crème de la crème, he also worked Stanley Cup playoffs and international hockey, in his case many a Canada Cup game. The only thing that separated D'Amico from just about everyone else was that he had the respect of the players and even the fans, so that he was never in hostile territory. That respect, coupled with his abilities, earned him induction into the Hockey Hall of Fame in 1993.

And like many a great player, D'Amico produced a son who followed in his footsteps. Son Angelo D'Amico lined his first NHL game in 2000, just like his old man. Like John, Angelo played hockey as a kid, but at a certain age realized that there was no future in the game for him as a player and made the move to officiating. Today, the name D'Amico still appears in game summaries, and although Angelo is the man so identified, it is a name that still evokes John, the Gordie Howe of the zebra set.

John LeClair

When he started to play well with Montreal, especially during the 1993 Cup Stanley finals, they called John LeClair the Mountain Man. In part, this was a nickname because of his size (6'3", 225 lbs.), in part because of his play (as a power forward), and in part because he was the first NHLer to have been born in Vermont (the only other Vermontian is Graham Mink who has played just a few games with Washington).

The Canadiens had liked him enough that in 1987, when he became draft eligible, they selected him 33rd overall. Amazingly, by that date, the only serious hockey LeClair had been involved in was with Bellows, a Vermont high school hardly known for producing NHLers the way St. Michael's in Toronto or Notre Dame in Wilcox did.

LeClair attended the University of Vermont that fall and for the next three and a half years developed into a bona fide player. He grew and gained strength, developed a hard-working attitude to go with a deadly shot and abrasive style of play, and when the Habs called him up near the end of the 1990-91 season, the 23-year-old was ready to play hockey.

He showed promise in his first two years with the Habs that went beyond what his actual contributions suggested, but 1992-93 was the start of something important for LeClair. He scored 19 goals during the regular season, and in the Stanley Cup finals he scored two successive overtime goals. In game three against Los Angeles, his goal just 34 seconds into the fourth period gave Montreal a 4-3 win and a 2-1 series lead. Two nights later, he did it again, scoring at 14:37 for a 3-2 win and a stranglehold on the series. The Habs closed out the victory in the next game, and LeClair was rightly given some of the credit for the Cup win.

The next year he had 19 goals again, but the year after he scored once in his first nine games, a slow start that cost him his place with the team. Montreal, a team known for smart drafting and patience in developing players, gave up on him, even though he was developing at a pace that was not unusual. The Habs sent him to Philadelphia in a blockbuster deal that saw Mark Recchi go from the Flyers to the Habs as the main elements of the exchange.

LeClair blossomed almost from the day he arrived in Philadelphia. He scored 25 goals in his 37 games with the team that year, and the next three years he had seasons of 51, 50, and 51 goals. Quickly this was called one of the worst trades in Montreal history. To make matters embarrassingly worse for the Habs, LeClair had the habit of scoring in bunches whenever his Flyers played his old team, a constant reminder of how poor the deal was for Montreal. Recchi settled into the Montreal lineup and became a solid 30-goal scorer, but LeClair flourished on the Legion of Doom line in Philly with Eric Lindros and Mikael Renberg and became a premier power forward in the game. Ironically, he also started to suffer serious injuries which kept him out of the lineup for extended periods, and he never won a Cup with the Flyers as he had with Montreal.

Nevertheless, LeClair's career came to be more defined by his play with Lindros than his early, developmental years with Montreal, but he is also the poster boy for a player exacting revenge on the team that traded him and proving time and again the deal, contrary to the alert work at the draft table years earlier, was made in error.

Ken Linseman

Long before Esa Tikkanen pested his way into the hearts and guts of hockey fans from coast to coast there was Ken Linseman, the man teammate Bobby Clarke called the Rat, not because of his style of play (which is the more appropriate reason) but because captain Clarke simply thought Linseman resembled a rat. Still, it was the Rat's gamesmanship that made his reputation. He would push and shove after whistles, slash the back of an opponent's leg just enough to sting but not enough to draw a penalty. Trash talking was another skill as was every other conceivable play intended to get a skilled player off his game.

Linseman was more than just a pest, though. He was the player teammates liked to play with and whom opponents hated to play against. He was the guy who angered and annoyed, and then scored the game-winning goal. He was never dominating enough to be called the best player on the team, but he had great speed and fine offensive talent. Indeed, when he was drafted by Philadelphia in 1978, he was referred to as the next Bobby Clarke, a weighty tag, indeed, for a 20-year-old.

The bigger issue after drafting him, however, was signing him. Linseman had played the previous season with Birmingham in the WHA as an 18-year-old, and the Bulls claimed they still owned his rights and would try to block any attempt by the Flyers to get him into the NHL without compensation. The case threatened to go to court as the Bulls and NHLPA executive director Alan Eagleson exchanged insults and curses trying to claim rights to the player.

Of course, a deal was reached and Linseman started his NHL career in Philly in 1978-79. After a few games, he was sent to the minors, but the team played poorly and replaced coach Bob McCammon with Pat Quinn. One of Quinn's first moves was to call up Linseman from the farm team, and the Rat never played another game in the minors. By his second year he scored 22 goals and irritated his way into a full-time job with the team. His skill was to get opponents so mad that they became distracted to the point of playing poorly. Another nickname? Shift disturber.

Unfortunately, Linseman never got more than 24 goals in his first four years with the Flyers, and this ensured that the comparisons to Bobby Clarke would end and his popularity compromised. He was traded to Edmonton in the summer of 1982 and immediately increased his output to 33 goals. The year after, while scoring less, he was part of the Oilers' first Stanley Cup triumph. General manager Glen Sather later traded Linseman to Boston for Mike Krushelnyski, and it was with the Bruins that Linseman had his longest stay, five and a half years. His new team faced the Oilers in the 1988 finals, losing badly. In 860 career games, Linseman averaged nearly a point a game and more than two penalty minutes a game, a rare combination of skill and abrasiveness. Linesman, however, lived on as a disruptive force for the rest of his career which ended with a two-game stint in Toronto in 1991-92.

Despite his talent, Linseman went through life in his own way and on his own terms. He liked painter Andrew Wyeth and novelist Ayn Rand—not typical interests for the average hockey player. He enjoyed casinos and stock markets, real estate and fast cars. He was well-rounded away from the rink and as such he was perhaps misunderstood off ice even though everyone on ice knew exactly what the Rat was all about.

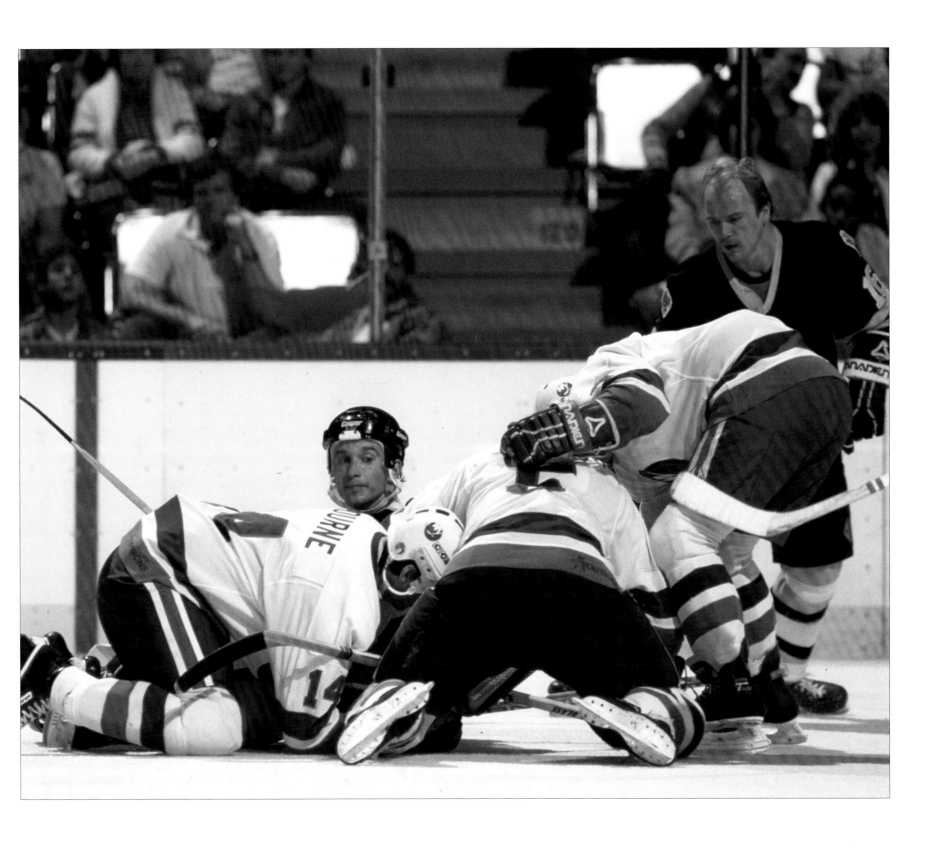

Lanny McDonald

He played his first game at the start of the 1973-74 season with Toronto. He played his last game the night the Stanley Cup was awarded to finish the 1988-89 season, with Calgary. In between, Lanny McDonald lived a dream, a dream that had records and magic moments, highs and lows, and a Cup triumph to end the dream in a magical world.

His first two seasons with the Leafs were rough. Drafted fourth overall in 1973, McDonald joined the team as a 20-year-old Prairie boy trying to make it big in the hockey capital. He scored just 14 and 17 goals, respectively, in those first two years, and fans let him know they expected more. In 1975-76, he delivered, catapulting to 37 goals and 93 points and developing into one of the best right wingers in the league. McDonald worked tirelessly on his wrist shot. His *pièce de resistance* was taking a pass as he crossed the blueline and letting fire a deadly snapshot or slapshot that beat the goalie to the far side or between the pads.

Teamed with best friend and centreman Darryl Sittler, the pair formed a line with left winger Errol Thompson. McDonald had three straight years of 46, 47, and 43 goals, and the team made it deep into the playoffs for the first time since winning the Cup in 1967. They were the most beloved athletes in the city, both for their skill on ice and their charisma, charitable work, and brotherly love off ice.

Leafs owner Harold Ballard enjoyed a ticklish relationship with his players, some of whom flourished under his reign, others of whom wilted. When the owner hired Punch Imlach as GM, Imlach traded McDonald to upset Sittler and try to re-kindle Sittler's energy. The strategy didn't work. Fans picketed outside Maple Leaf Gardens calling for McDonald's return. Sittler tore the "C" off his sweater. The chemistry of a team so close to the Cup was destroyed.

McDonald spent a year and a half in Colorado with the hopeless Rockies and then was traded to Calgary where he played the last seven and a half seasons of his career. In 1982-83, he scored an incredible 66 goals with that slap shot down the right wing move, and as he got older and his scoring diminished he became a greater leader and inspiration to younger players who were forming a winning core in Calgary.

In the final weeks of his career, McDonald achieved three Hall of Fame-quality milestones. On March 21, 1989, he scored his 500th goal. He played just four more regular season games and he remains the player to score his 500th closest to the end of his career. Just two weeks earlier, on March 7, he scored a goal for his 1,000th career point.

In the 1989 playoffs, the team was so deep in talent that he didn't play every night. The proud 36-year-old knew the end was near. In the final game of the season, game six of the Cup finals in Montreal, captain Lanny McDonald was in the lineup. With the game tied 1-1 early in the second period, McDonald scored the final goal of his career to give the Flames a 2-1 lead they never relinquished. They won 4-2 and became the first visiting team to win the Cup on Montreal ice. NHL president John Ziegler came on the ice to hand the Stanley Cup off to the Flames' captain, McDonald, and a career that was at its apex was also at its end in the same moment. Once McDonald got to the dressing room, tears mixed with champagne, he retired. Gentleman and champion both.

Mario Lemieux

The second retirement, on January 25, 2006, seemed to make more sense than the first one, but as a result hurt much more than the first.

When Mario Lemieux retired in the spring of 1997 after Pittsburgh had been eliminated by Philadelphia in the first round of the playoffs, he was just 31 years old. He said he was tired of playing, tired of fighting through centre-ice interference, tired of hooking, holding, clutching, grabbing, all the offenses which were taking the skill out of a game created to celebrate skill.

Lemieux became owner of the Penguins, a team that had drafted him in 1984 and the only team he had ever played for. He tried to improve the team on ice, through smart hockey moves, and to improve its fortunes as a business enterprise by getting a new arena built. Once Maple Leaf Gardens hosted its last game in February 1999, the Penguins' arena, affectionately known as the Igloo, became the oldest NHL building at a time when every city was financing a new arena with luxury boxes, state-of-the-art broadcasting and hosting facilities, and many other features needed to maximize revenue in the dollar era of the game.

By the time he retired, Mario had scored more than 600 goals, won two Stanley Cups, six Art Ross Trophies, and countless other awards and honours. When he came into the NHL as an 18-year-old, it took him mere seconds to score his first goal. He was as natural a scorer as the game had ever seen. When he said goodbye in 1997, it was clear that he was still every bit the superstar from his first shift to his last.

His career was hardly straightforward, however. He missed much of two seasons with a bad back, much of two more fighting Hodgkin's disease. Yet where most people recover to live and breathe, he recovered to score goals with the same apparent ease. He was unbelievable, spectacular, awe-inspiring, all in one.

Midway through the 2000-01 season, Lemieux came out of retirement. He missed the game, he said, and he wanted his kids to have the chance to see him play. He thought if he returned the franchise would be more valuable and this in turn would make it easier to finance a new arena. In his first game back, just before Christmas, it took him mere seconds to score again. It was as if three days, not three and a half years, had elapsed since he last touched the puck.

The new Mario was the same player on ice from afar, but inside he was a radically different person. He was more accommodating with the media. He played for the love of his family. He played as an owner and looked at the game with the dual perspective of goals and assists and also bottom lines. The new Mario could still dominate the game, but he realized more fully his place in the game's consciousness. When he retired in 1997, he had passed up the chance to play at the 1996 World Cup for Team Canada. Upon his return, he was delighted to assume the captaincy and guide Canada to the 2002 Olympics.

Lemieux's calm and confident demeanour was a huge contributing factor to Canada's gold medal. There was his two-goal performance against Dominik Hasek and the Czechs in the preliminary round to make it clear Hasek would work no magic against Canada as he had four years earlier in a shootout. There was his brilliant fake-acceptance of a pass that gave Paul Kariya an open net in the gold-medal game. But as important, there was his presence, his even keel, his aura of success. He had it again a year and a half later at the 2006 World Cup, his last great hurrah. And then he retired again, finally. If not the greatest of all time, then top five. No doubt.

The Game

Mark Messier

The events are part of hockey history now, part of Stanley Cup lore and New York sports mythology. But at the time, it was merely words meeting deeds head on.

The 1994 playoffs were going well for the New York Rangers as they headed into their Conference finals series against New Jersey. The Rangers swept aside rivals the Islanders in four games to start their chase for the Cup and followed with a relatively easy elimination of Washington in five games.

The Devils had the tougher time, fending off Buffalo 2-1 in game seven of their first-round matchup and squeaking by Boston in six games in the next round. In the Rangers-Devils series, teams split the first two games at Madison Square Garden, and the Rangers took the series lead with a 3-2 win in double overtime of game three.

The Devils took control, however, with a 3-1 win in game four and then a key 4-1 victory in game five. They headed home to the Meadowlands with a chance to eliminate the Blueshirts. Rangers captain Mark Messier would have none of it, though. "We know we have to win it," he said of game six the day previous at practice. "We can win it, and we are going to win it."

For most of two periods in that game, however, Messier's words seemed merely like more prattle from a superstar using the media to make his point. The Rangers were trailing 2-0, and Messier was having a lousy game. Then coach Mike Keenan decided to put all his eggs in one basket and loaded his first line with Messier, Alexei Kovalev, and Steve Larmer. The move worked.

Late in the second period, Messier dropped the puck to Kovalev deep in the New Jersey end, and Kovalev's shot beat Brodeur to make it 2-1 after 40 minutes. Early in the third period, Messier took his promise to heart. He beat Brodeur after taking a cross-ice pass from defenceman Brian Leetch and beat the goalie to the far side with a bullet shot to tie the game. Later in the period, he converted a rebound off a Leetch shot that Brodeur couldn't control to give the Rangers a 3-2 lead. And then, to complete the hat trick, salt the victory, and earn a place in history, he intercepted a pass deep in his own end in the final minute and shot the puck the length of the ice into the empty net. Three goals, one assist, a 4-2 victory.

Still, Messier's work was not done. The Rangers led game seven 1-0 with less than a minute to play, but New Jersey tied the score with Brodeur on the bench for the extra attacker. In the dressing room before the first overtime, Messier talked to the players. He talked and talked until they forgot about the bad goal and focused on winning in extra time, which they did in the second OT.

They were off to the finals, and once there they defeated Vancouver 3-2 in game seven to win the Cup for the first time since 1940. The hero was Messier, not so much for his performance in the finals but for his guaranteed win. That's what heroes are made of.

Mats Sundin

Ever since he was 17 years old, Mats Sundin has represented his country with pride, so much so that his international career has overshadowed a fine NHL career.

Sundin played for Sweden at the 1990 World Junior Championship and just a few months later for Tre Kronor at the senior World Championship in Switzerland. Although he had a good rookie season in the NHL in 1990-91 with the Quebec Nordiques, he became a national hero back home for his performance at the '91 World Championship in Finland.

In the final game against the Soviet Union to decide gold, Sundin broke a 1-1 third period tie with one of the greatest goals in Swedish hockey history. He burst down the right wing, made a dazzling outside-in move on the defenceman, and scored on a perfect backhand shot. The defenceman he beat? Slava Fetisov.

Back in the NHL, Sundin had four excellent years with Quebec, establishing himself as one of the bright young stars from Europe playing in the league. He had been the first European ever to be selected first overall at the Entry Draft, and here he was, game in-game out, living up to expectations. In 1992-93, he had 114 points, and looked to be on his way to superstardom.

But the Nordiques decided that acquiring Wendel Clark from the Leafs was worth the price of sacrificing Sundin. Clark had had a career year in Toronto, scoring 46 goals in 64 games, and his popularity in Toronto increased his value significantly. Sundin, nervous about coming to Toronto, phoned his boyhood idol and compatriot, Borje Salming, for advice. Salming told the young star to go to Toronto and play well. The rest would take care of itself.

Now with eleven seasons to his Leafs' credit, Sundin has been an enigmatic star and disappointment both. He has produced 30 goals nearly every season, averaged better than a point a game, and helped the team make the playoffs consistently. In 1999, he became the first non-Canadian to captain the historic franchise, and his conduct on ice and off in this duty has been impeccable. But, of course, he has not brought the city the Stanley Cup, the one prize Leafs fans covet more than any other.

At every opportunity, however, he has played for Sweden with equal pride and greater success. He played at the 1991 Canada Cup, 1996 World Cup, and 2004 World Cup. In 1996, he was likely the best forward in the competition. He has played for Tre Kronor at all three NHL-driven Olympics—1998, 2002, 2006—culminating last February in a gold medal victory with a win over Finland in the final game. Sundin assisted on Nicklas Lidstrom's game-winning goal.

He has also participated in the World Championships on several occasions since his 1991 heroics—1992 (gold), 1994 (bronze), 1998 (gold), 2001 (bronze), 2003 (silver). In 2003, he was named tournament MVP. In all, he has played in 12 major senior international tournaments since 1991, more than any other superstar player of his generation. Now if he can only bring the Cup to Toronto, his place in history will be forever forged among the greatest of the greats!

Mike Bossy

22 Bossy
50 in 50

At the time, few records were as sacred as Maurice Richard's historic achievement of scoring 50 goals in 50 games in 1944-45. True, many of the top goalies were off to war and many teams were depleted by lack of skilled players because of the war. But when the NHL expanded to 12 teams in 1967 and onward to 21 by 1980, there were many teams short on talent yet no one matched 50 in 50. Back in '44-'45, to illustrate how amazing the 50-in-50 feat was, the second top scorer was Boston's Herb Cain with just 32 goals.

Richard's record withstood the primes of some pretty amazing scorers. Gordie Howe, "Boom Boom" Geoffrion, Bobby Hull, Frank Mahovlich, Phil Esposito, Guy Lafleur. They were the greatest scorers of their various generations, but they never had 50 goals in 50 games. Then Mike Bossy came along. As a rookie in 1977-78, he scored 53 times. The next year, he led the league with 69 goals. The year after, he "dipped" to 51, but his New York Islanders won their first Stanley Cup with a team so skilled and young it seemed destined to stay at the top for a long time.

As the 50th game of the '80-'81 season approached, Bossy had company in chasing the Richard record. Charlie Simmer of Los Angeles was scoring at a greater rate. Simmer had 39 goals in 38 games while Bossy was 38 goals for 39 games. Simmer slowed down as number 50 approached, though, and at the 48-game mark he had 46 goals. After 49 games, he still had 46 goals.

Bossy accelerated toward the record thanks to a hat trick in game number 47, scoring his 46th, 47th, and 48th goals and leaving him with three games to score twice. That hat trick was his eighth of the season, a new NHL record that had been held by Joe Malone, Rick Martin, and Phil Esposito. His seventh hat trick came the previous game when he scored four times.

In game 48, the Islanders won easily, 5-0 over Calgary, but Flames' goalie Rejean Lemelin would have none of this 50-in-50 talk at his doorstep. He stopped Bossy point blank twice, and the sniper remained at 48 goals after as many games.

Game 49 was another win, 3-0 over Detroit, but Bossy again fired blanks, most notably on an empty net as the Red Wings pressed to score with the game 2-0 and within reach. It all came down to a date with the Quebec Nordiques the night of January 24, 1981.

That afternoon, Bossy watched the Kings and Boston play a matinee game. Simmer needed four goals to get to 50-in-50 first. Incredibly, he scored three times to reach the 50-game mark with 49 goals, one shy of the record. The record was there for Bossy to tie.

The Quebec goalie that night against the Islanders was Ron Grahame, and, as was the case the previous two games, coach Al Arbour played Bossy as much as humanly possible. Yet through 55 minutes of the game, Bossy was still goalless and had all but given up on the Rocket's record. Then, at 15:50, Bossy's backhand shot in close beat Grahame and he became energized. He remained on the ice almost the rest of the game. Less than three minutes later, he took a pass from linemate Bryan Trottier, and like he had done a million times before, he one-timed a quick snapshot on goal. It eluded a sliding Grahame and hit the net. Fifty goals in 50 games for the first time in 36 years!

Mike Bullard

How times change. As a rookie in 1981-82, Mike Bullard was paid the princely sum of $65,000. In 1991-92, his last year in the NHL, Bullard signed with the Leafs for $700,000 over two years. His was a career that sped into the fast lane and careened into the wall more than once, but his 51 goals in '83-'84 put him in elite company.

Bullard had shown great promise in '81-'82 by scoring 36 goals, but his progress stalled the next year when he suffered a prolonged bout of mononucleosis and missed more than a quarter of the season. His production dipped to 22 goals, but the following year everything went right. In his case, that meant being given the confidence of coach Lou Angotti who gave Bullard plenty of ice time playing five-on-five as well as extra duty killing penalties and on the power play. The result was 51 goals and superstar status.

Just as things looked bright, though, they went dark. Angotti was replaced by Bob Berry, and the Penguins drafted Mario Lemieux in the summer of 1984. Of course, Mario made the team right away, and Berry gave the teenage star all the ice time and the skilled linemates. Bullard had been named captain that same summer, but his production dipped to 32 goals and star talk was replaced by trade talk. To make matters worse, he hurt his back, which negatively affected his play, and he was arrested for drunk driving in January '85 which only served to hurt his reputation further. A month later, he was fined for missing curfew.

Bullard rebounded the next year, but tensions with Berry could not be worked through. Bullard felt he was now being ignored for the more talented Lemieux; Berry called him weak defensively and a poor team player. To wit, even when he scored 51 goals, Bullard was a -33 in plus/minus stats, one of the worst ratings in the league. In his five full seasons with the team, he was a cumulative -114.

One day early in the '86-'87 season, he and Berry had a heated fight during practice. The next day Bullard was stripped of his captaincy, and in response he left the team demanding a trade. The Pens happily obliged and Bullard was sent to Calgary for Dan Quinn who had had a tough start to the new year with the Flames.

The trade motivated Bullard. He had a good remainder of the season with Calgary and the next year had the best statistics of his career, scoring 48 goals and 103 points playing right wing on a skilled line with Jim Peplinski and Joel Otto. Coach Bob Johnson moved the centreman to the wing to utilize the player's speed and shot while minimizing his defensive play which was more important for a centre to master than a winger.

After a stint in St. Louis, Bullard wound up in Philadelphia come the 1989 playoffs. The team went to the Conference finals, the closest he ever came to the Stanley Cup. In fact, although he played more than 700 regular-season games, Bullard played just 40 more in the post-season. Before and after his final shot with the Leafs, though (which lasted just one year and a scant 14 goals), Bullard became a mainstay in the German league for a decade, scoring plenty of goals along the way, just like he did in 1983-84.

Montreal vs. Calgary

Les Canadiens and Les Flames met in the Stanley Cup finals twice in the 1980s, Montreal prevailing in 1986 in game five in Calgary, the Flames winning in Montreal in 1989 in the penultimate game. The Calgary victory was doubly sweet: it was the first time the franchise had won the Cup, and it was the first time ever that Montreal lost the Cup on home ice.

The Flames had a tougher time getting to the finals in 1986. They beat St. Louis 2-1 in game seven of their Conference finals while Montreal dispatched the Rangers in five easier games. In the finals, Calgary won the opening game at home, 5-2. It was to be their only win of the series. Montreal evened the series 1-1 with a dramatic 3-2 win in overtime. Brian Skrudland set an NHL record by scoring just nine seconds into the fourth period, and the Flames never recovered from the psychological effects of this rapid-fire loss.

In game three, Calgary had a 2-1 lead late in the first period, but Montreal scored at 18:25, 19:17, and 19:33 to take a 4-2 lead into the dressing room. In the second, Calgary drew to within a goal, but Ulf Dahlin scored another late-period goal, this at 19:22, and the Flames were out of rallies this night, falling 5-3.

Game four was another close one, a mere 1-0 victory thanks to a Claude Lemieux goal midway through the third and a solid performance by Patrick Roy. Game five, back in Calgary, was anti-climactic. Montreal built a 4-1 lead, and two Calgary goals made the game closer than it was. Rookie Patrick Roy was named Conn Smythe Trophy winner, and the Habs won their 22nd Stanley Cup.

The 1989 finals was a different beast altogether. In the intervening years the Flames made a number of vital roster moves, trading Brett Hull to St. Louis for veteran defenceman Rob Ramage, getting young Theo Fleury into the lineup, and adding all-stars such as Doug Gilmour and Joe Nieuwendyk to the team. In all, Calgary had just nine players on the team that were in the '86 finals; Montreal had 14.

The roster changes made a world of difference for the Flames. After a 2-2 first period in game one of the '89 finals, for instance, it was the rookie Fleury who scored the only goal of the second, a goal that stood as the game winner after 60 minutes. Fleury had been called up midway through the year and played so well that he never went back.

As in 1986, Montreal came back to win game two, this time by a 4-2 count. The Habs scored the only two goals of the third to break a 2-2 tie, and they put the pressure on even more in game three with a 4-3 win in double overtime. Ryan Walter was the hero late in the fifth period of that game, but it was a tough, violent game from start to finish, one that brought the Flames together. They evened the series at the Forum with a 4-2 win in game four, Al MacInnis scoring a late third-period goal which proved to be the back-breaker for Montreal.

Game five showed the Flames to be in Cup mode. Joel Otto scored just 28 seconds from the opening faceoff, and it was a late-period goal on the power play by MacInnis that gave the Flames a commanding 3-1 lead. Goalie Mike Vernon was outstanding in net and the Flames won 3-2. Game six was the clincher. It has become a part of Calgary history for so many reasons. With the game tied 1-1 early in the second, Lanny McDonald scored to give the Flames a 2-1 lead. It was to be the final goal in his final NHL game for the longtime captain, and the Flames never lost the lead.

Gilmour added a third Calgary goal, swatting the puck out of midair beside Roy in the Montreal goal, and Gilmour added another into the empty net to salt away the 4-2 win. It was the culmination of a great mini-rivalry and a great run for the Flames which had spent much of the decade fighting a losing battle against the more talented Oilers. Still, in 1989, they got their championship and earned their place in Stanley Cup history.

Montreal vs. Quebec

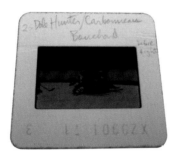

There are very few pure rivalries in hockey. Toronto-Montreal is not only the oldest, but in many ways it is the defining rivalry of the game because it pits English Canada against French Canada. Within the cultural landscape of Quebec, however, the Montreal-Quebec rivalry that flourished in the 1980s might well have been more important and certainly was as violent and emotional as any series of games between any two teams in any sport in history.

The rivalry raged for 16 years, from the time the Nordiques joined the NHL in 1979 to the time the team was tragically transferred to Denver, Colorado, in the summer of 1995. During that decade and a half, the Habs and Nords experienced differing levels of success. The Habs were a consistently strong team while Quebec was sometimes as good, sometimes much worse. Quebec missed the playoffs its first year, then made the post-season for seven straight years, missed the playoffs for the next six out of seven seasons, and then were back in it in 1994-95 as it developed into a Stanley Cup contender.

The rivalry featured some of the most intense playoff series in the NHL's long and storied chase for the Stanley Cup. In a nutshell, it began in 1982 when Quebec won the opening round best-of-five, 3-2 in games. In 1984, Montreal won a best-of-seven in six games in the division finals. In 1985, Quebec prevailed in seven games of the division finals, and in 1987 the result was reversed. The last playoff meeting was 1993, a mere addendum to the history, when the Nordiques lost in six games of the opening round. So, the teams played just five rounds of playoff hockey, but coupled with war-like goings on during the regular season, these were games for the ages.

The rivalry had many parts to it. Quebec City never forgave Montreal for stealing Jean Beliveau from it. In fact, the antipathy grew worse a generation later when Guy Lafleur went from junior hockey in Quebec City to Montreal to play in the NHL (Quebec got the last laugh, though, as Lafleur finished his career with the Nordiques in 1990-91 after a Hall of Fame career with the Canadiens).

In almost three full seasons starting in 1979, the Nordiques never lost to Montreal at home—and the Habs never lost to the Nordiques at home, either! The rosters of the two warring teams spoke volumes about the era. Montreal had Lafleur, Guy Carbonneau, Claude Lemieux, Pierre Mondou, Robert Picard. The Nordiques had Michel Goulet, Real Cloutier, Wilf Paiement, Pierre Lacroix, Pierre Aubry.

Without a doubt, though, it was the epic brawls in 1984 that still crystallize what hockey meant to those two teams and how important was beating the other team. It was game six of the division finals, April 20, 1984, Montreal trailing 2-0 at the end of the second period. Before the teams headed to the dressing room, Dale Hunter of Quebec ran into Montreal goalie Steve Penney. Louis Sleigher (Quebec) and Jean Hamel started fighting, and every player on both teams was on the ice duking it out.

Eventually order was restored, but the officials didn't figure out all the penalties until the start of the third. By that time many players who were to receive game misconducts were back on the ice to stretch prior to the start of the period, and further mayhem ensued when Chris Nilan (Montreal) started fighting anew with Randy Moller who had jumped Chris Chelios. Another full-scale brawl erupted, another round of game misconducts. Montreal rallied with five goals to win the game 5-3 and eliminate the Nordiques, but not before a hockey war of untold proportions had unfolded. Today, brawling is gone and so are the Nordiques, but the Montreal-Quebec rivalry remains one of the game's greatest losses in the NHL's history.

U.S. College Hockey

A generation previous to this, U.S. college hockey was hardly on the radar of coaches, scouts, and general managers of NHL teams. Quickly, though, the American university system with its scholarship offers successfully lured many Canadian and American kids to a place where they could get a free education and develop their hockey skills at the same time. If the hockey worked out, they could leave any time. If it didn't, they were well prepared for a job in the working world.

The 1990-91 NCAA hockey season, in retrospect, is chock full of names that became household just a few years later. The year ended with Northern Michigan beating Maine in the semi-finals (pictured here) and Boston University in a wild 8-7 triple overtime victory in the finals after trailing 3-0 in the first period. It was their first national championship. The team was led by Hobey Baker Award winner and Final Four MVP, Scott Beattie, and another centreman, Dallas Drake. The defence was anchored by Hobey Baker runner-up, Brad Werenka, who played for Canada at the 1994 Olympics.

Northern Michigan played in the WCHA (Western Collegiate Hockey Association) which also boasted alumni Ben Hankinson, Tom Pederson, and Chris McAlpine. The Boston University team from Hockey East that they beat included a top line of Shawn McEachern, Keith Tkachuk, and Tony Amonte, all familiar names to fans of the NHL.

The 1991 East All-America team featured Joe Juneau on the second team (RPI), Pete Ciavaglia (Harvard), and Jim Montgomery (Maine). Montgomery became a teammate of Paul Kariya with the Black Bears and won a national championship in 1993. Jean-Yves Roy (also Maine) and Les Kuntar (St. Lawrence) were on the first team.

Doug Weight played for Lake Superior State and helped the team win its CCHA championship. That school, led by coach of the year Jeff Jackson, beat Michigan 6-5 in the final game. The Wolverines had Mike Eastwood as a forward and Steve Shields and Darrin Madeley in goal and were coached by longtime NHLer Red Berenson. Berenson remains with the team after a quarter of a century and boasts one of the most successful college records of all time.

The ECAC also featured the likes of Ted Donato (Harvard), Dan Ratushny (Cornell), John LeClair (Vermont), and Craig Conroy (Clarkson). Hockey East included Amonte (BU) and Rob Gaudreau and Chris Therien (both of Providence).

Coaches also featured prominently. In addition to Berenson, there was Ron Anderson at Merrimack and Shawn Walsh at Maine. Ben Smith was coach at Northeastern. Smith later made his mark more importantly as coach of the USA National Women's team that won gold at the 1998 Olympics, silver in 2002, and bronze in 2006.

This was just the tip of the iceberg. As the pro game has gotten more competitive, and as the young men who aspire to play pro have gotten more savvy, American colleges have become increasingly important to players for both education and hockey development. As the 21st century began, it also became an important place for women to go as well, the only true amateur alternate to NWHL play in Canada and as such a place where some European women have gone to develop their playing skills.

Nick
Fotiu

He may appear to have been a fighter and not much else, but Nick Fotiu managed to stay in the NHL for 13 years so there has to be more than meets the eye. The typical euphemism is that the team fighter is "good in the dressing room," but in Fotiu's case it was both bang-on true and also as far from the truth as possible. Fotiu was the king of practical jokes, a player who spent what seemed like his every waking hour getting teammates and team personnel in a variety of embarrassing and angering situations.

Fotiu was the first native of New York City to play for the Rangers. Like the Mullen brothers, he learned hockey on the blacktop of Staten Island, playing roller hockey and developing his skills in Cape Cod on the side. He made his Rangers' debut in 1976 after two years with New England in the WHA, and while he fought the tough guys on other teams to protect his own superstars, he was driving his teammates crazy in the dressing room and on road trips.

Phil Esposito hated cockroaches. Fotiu made this discovery and got into the habit of putting them in Espo's equipment or clothes. When he opened the bag, Espo screamed with upset because he was so meticulous he couldn't understand how the roaches would find their way into his belongings. Espo once brought his brand new, white gold shoes into the room. Fotiu, in an inspired moment, spray-painted them orange.

On one road trip, he shared a room with Bill Goldsworthy. When Goldsworthy slept, Fotiu went to the hotel lobby and plucked a giant lobster from the aquarium. He put it on Goldsworthy's chest, and the player woke up screaming in terror. The next morning, Fotiu got up first and hid in the closet. Goldsworthy awoke and went to get his jacket only to feel Fotiu's arms as he reached for the hanger. More screams.

Some teammates went to breakfast at a diner one morning. Fotiu finished first and left quickly, but on his way out he noticed that goalie John Davidson's truck was parked beside a garbage dump. Fotiu covered the truck with the refuse, but later that night Davidson and friends reciprocated when they covered Fotiu's house, trees, and shrubs with toilet paper.

Fotiu loved to replace whipped cream with shaving cream and put powder in the team's blow dryers in the dressing room. He locked players' suitcases on road trips and kept the keys. He kept everyone on their toes and made sure for every angry face there were 20 others laughing. On ice, Fotiu was most popular during the pre-game skate when he'd toss pucks into the crowd before heading off. During games, he skated hard, hit harder, and did his best to irritate the opposition. He was so well loved in New York that when he returned to Madison Square Garden as a member of the Hartford Whalers, fans brought signs saying, "Bring Back Nick!"

And the Rangers did just that, re-acquiring him less than two years after letting him go to the Whalers in the Expansion Draft of 1979. Fotiu ended his playing days skating briefly for Calgary, Philadelphia, and Edmonton, but the man who grew up on the streets of New York remained a New Yorker through and through. He wasn't the most talented player to pass through the league, but his inclusion in the league on and off ice was entertaining nonetheless.

Edmonton Oilers 1990

In many ways, the fifth and final Stanley Cup by the Edmonton Oilers in 1990 was the most satisfying. No matter how optimistic the players, it was impossible to think a Cup was possible at the start of this 1989-90 season given the circumstances. In the summer of 1988, Wayne Gretzky was traded to Los Angeles. He was clearly the best player in the world and the main contributor to the team's four championships between 1984 and 1988. How could the team win without him?

Furthermore, in the previous spring's playoffs, it was Gretzky who led the Kings to a stunning, seven-game victory over the Oilers in the opening round of the playoffs. If any team were to be considered Cup contenders, it was Gretzky and his high-flying Kings moreso than the Gretzky-less Oilers.

The 1990 playoffs, however, might have been Mark Messier's finest moment. He led the team to a perilously close seven-game win over perpetual losers Winnipeg Jets in the first round, while out west Gretzky was leading the Kings to a six-game win over Calgary to set up another LA-Edmonton showdown, this in round two of the post-season.

Number 99 could not work his magic against his old club a second time. The Oilers won the first game 7-0 to eradicate Gretzky's ghost once and for all from the psyches of the Edmonton players. They were equally dominant in game two, winning 6-1, and although the next two games were close, the old Edmonton firewagon hockey outgunned Gretzky 5-4 and 6-5 to advance with a convincing four-game sweep.

The Oilers had a tougher time in the Conference finals, beating Chicago in six games to set up a showdown against Boston which had advanced with a four-game sweep over Washington. It was the battle of goalies in one sense, the Oilers having acquired Bill Ranford from the Bruins for Andy Moog a short time ago. But, it was also another test for the more experienced Oilers' team. No, they didn't have Gretzky, but they had Messier, Glenn Anderson, Randy Gregg, Jari Kurri, Esa Tikkanen and 12 players in all who had won in 1988.

Boston's best chance of proving its point was in game one, but the Bruins lost 3-2 thanks to a goal by Petr Klima late in the third period of overtime. It was a painful loss for Boston because the team had rallied with two goals in the third, the second at 18:31, to force overtime in the first place. Game two was a waltz for Edmonton, 7-2, and the Oilers went back to Alberta with a commanding two-game lead in the series.

The Bruins won the third game, 2-1, showing some character by jumping out to a 2-0 first-period lead and hanging on for the win, but any hopes of a rally were extinguished two nights later when Anderson scored twice in the first to get the Oilers off on the right foot. They cruised to a 5-1 win and headed to Boston with a 3-1 series lead. The Cup would be in the building for game five, and they had no intention of passing up the chance to win the hallowed trophy for a fifth time.

Despite the overflow and partisan crowd at the tiny Garden in downtown Boston, the Oilers took the drama out of the game and never gave the Bruins much of a chance to gain momentum and make the fans a factor. After a scoreless opening 20 minutes, Anderson scored early in the second and Craig Simpson scored midway through the period to give the Oilers a 2-0 lead. They scored twice more in the third before Lyndon Byers put the Bruins on the board, but the game ended with a decisive 4-1 win by the visitors.

As Messier held the Cup aloft and his veteran teammates surrounded him, the beautiful reality emerged that hockey is more a team game than a game that can be won by any individual. Great as Gretzky was, he couldn't take the Kings to the Cup by himself. And great as he was, his individual loss by the Oilers could be made up for through superior team play. Even after all the glory of the 1980s, this victory in the spring of 1990 might well have been the defining moment in Edmonton's hockey history.

Owen Nolan

Hockey: Quebec Nordiques Owen Nolan #11 in action vs NY Islanders Rich Pilon #47;

X47839 TK01 F08 001

Owen Nolan was selected first overall by the Quebec Nordiques in 1990 on the strength of two years in the OHL with Cornwall. In the first, he averaged about a point a game and spent 213 minutes in the penalty box. In the second, he virtually doubled his point production and spent 240 minutes in the box.

The Nordiques were drawn to him because of his size, strength, and soft hands. Because they had the first choice, they could have selected Jaromir Jagr (who went fifth, to Pittsburgh), Martin Brodeur (20th, New Jersey), Mike Ricci (4th, Philadelphia), or Keith Primeau (3rd, Detroit).

Nolan made the team out of training camp as an 18-year-old, but his first season was among the worst rookie seasons ever by a first-overall choice. He had trouble adjusting to the speed of the game. He wasn't the physically dominant player in a league of adults that he had been with the teenager set in junior hockey. He lacked the intensity and spark he played with in Cornwall. In 59 games, he scored a measly three goals and was a -19 in the plus/minus statistics.

Year two was different, though. Over that summer of 1991, Nolan dedicated himself to improving in all areas, came to camp in tremendous shape, and started the year like a veteran superstar. He ended the year with 42 goals and 73 points to his credit and looked to be rounding into shape as a true number-one pick. The next year, he scored 36 times but finished with more points (77), and the team made the playoffs now that it had Nolan and another young star, Joe Sakic.

Nolan's '93-'94 season ended almost before it began, though. He suffered a serious shoulder surgery in just his sixth game of the year, and that was it for him. He rebounded the following season by scoring 30 goals in 46 games during the lockout-shortened year, but early in '95-'96, when the team moved to Colorado, he was traded to San Jose straight up for Sandis Ozolinsh.

It was a shocking trade given his status, and a clear sign that the Avalanche felt he would never become a dominant player. In his first two years with the Sharks, he averaged 30 goals and then tapered off, recovering his form only in 1999-2000, his last year before free agency, when he scored 44 times.

The Sharks re-signed him prior to the new season at a huge raise from his early days. When he joined Quebec in 1990, Nolan signed a five-year deal that paid him $1,280,000. In 2000, he signed a staggering six-year, $36.5 million deal.

Unfortunately for the Sharks, Nolan settled in to be a comfortable, 23-goal man for the next three years and with that middling performance the Sharks traded him to Toronto where his career went further awry thanks to injuries, notably a back problem that forced him to miss all of 2005-06. The promise of greatness as a teen, teased by bursts of spectacular play in the NHL, gave way to mid-level play for much of his career.

Pat Verbeek

The name Pat Verbeek conjures up absolutely no grand recollections of end-to-end rushes, great one-timers, give-and-go spectacular plays, highlight-reel goals. Nothing. Yet, by the time the diminutive "Little Ball of Hate" (his Rangers' nickname) retired in 2002, he had amassed 522 goals, nearly 1,100 career points (1,063), and nearly triple the number of penalty minutes (2,905). All that's left to answer is, 'How did he do that?'

A native of Sarnia, Verbeek was a fine player with the Sudbury Wolves in the OHL before being drafted by lowly New Jersey in 1982. He made his debut with the Devils during the '82-'83 season at age 18 when he had five points in six games, and the next year he made the team full-time out of training camp. He never played a game in the minors.

After two fine seasons to start his career, Verbeek almost saw his career come to an end before it got off the ground. It was the summer of 1985, and he was back home helping his family work the farm. Verbeek slipped while he reached into a fertilizer bin to remove a piece of paper he feared might clog the machine. He fell into a corn-planting machine, and the auger sliced off his left thumb and damaged three other digits. He and his brother, Brian, went to the hospital, but it was Pat who had to give directions because Brian didn't know how to get there. En route, the car ran out of gas and they needed more help just to get to St. Joseph's Hospital in nearby Sarnia. Once there, the doctor asked Pat to see the thumb in the hopes it could be re-attached. Pat had figured there was no hope and had left it behind! He called his father who then searched through the four fertilizer bins until he found it. Gerry Verbeek then put it on ice and drove like mad to the hospital, and after five hours of microsurgery Dr. Brian Evans considered the job complete with the caveat that the process had about a 25% success rate.

Verbeek made a full recovery and scored 25 goals that season. He also lived up to his reputation as an agitator and horrible player to play against, which was fine by him. In the coming years he managed four seasons with at least 40 goals and four more of at least 30 goals. He liked to boast that most of those scores came in close, on second and third tries, knocking home a loose puck or a rebound, deflecting a shot off his butt or back. They weren't necessarily pretty, but a goal was a goal.

After playing more than six years with the Devils, Verbeek was traded to Hartford in 1989 where he stayed five and a half years. It wasn't until 1999, though, when the 34-year-old was in his 17th season, that he finally won the Stanley Cup for the first time, with Dallas. Just days later, he became a free agent and rejected a one-year offer, going to Detroit for two years instead. He never won a Stanley Cup with the Wings, but he retired a happy man in 2002.

Verbeek played in only two All-Star Games, never won an individual trophy and never made an end-of-year all-star team. Yet his statistics rank him among the greatest players to have passed through the NHL. While stats aren't everything, they are something. Now, only time will tell whether they are enough to get the pesky, determined forward into the Hockey Hall of Fame.

Patrick Roy

The older brother of Stephane Roy, who played a dozen games for the Minnesota North Stars in 1987-88, Patrick Roy hit the NHL ground running in 1985 when he began his Hall of Fame career.

He came to the Habs more or less directly from Granby, one of the worst teams in the Quebec major junior league, a team that gave Roy all the practice a goalie could hope for. Montreal, a franchise blessed with great goalies over the years, was in search of a new superstar and called Roy up to test his mettle. He ended up playing more than half the regular season in '85-'86, and in the playoffs he was not only the team's starting goalie, he was utterly unbeatable.

During the regular season, Roy's GAA was a middling 3.35. In the playoffs, he nearly halved that number to 1.92. Most impressive, though, was Roy's record under pressure, namely overtime. He won all three games the Habs played in OT, notably a 2-1 win over Hartford in game seven of the division finals, a series Montreal came perilously close to losing. Roy earned the Conn Smythe Trophy for his heroics and earned the moniker Saint Patrick from media and fans. Of course, this being Montreal, he also earned intensified pressure the next year, everyone expecting he'd now take the team to the Cup every year.

He couldn't perform this miracle, of course, but he had pretty close to a perfect season in '88-'89. He had a record of 33-5-6 in the regular season and took the team to the finals before losing to Calgary in six games. The trouble was that, apart from Roy, the Habs teams of these years weren't particularly good. They had no game-breaking scorer, no Big Three on defence a la Robinson-Savard-Lapointe, no two-way Selke greats to watch the other team's best players. There was Roy and the rest of the team.

Scintillating as he was as a kid in 1986, Roy's defining moment came seven years later when he took the Habs to another unexpected triumph. In the opening round of the 1993 playoffs, the Habs faced their provincial rivals in Quebec, the last playoff meeting between the natural rivals. The Nordiques won the opening game in overtime, 3-2, but Montreal fought back to win four of the next five and eliminate the Nordiques in six games. Two of those wins also came in overtime, starting the greatest OT performance in NHL history.

Montreal faced Buffalo in the division finals. The Habs won the first game 4-3 in regulation time and then reeled off three straight one-goal wins in overtime, all by 4-3 scores. Roy had now won five straight OT games. In the conference finals, against the Rangers, Montreal won in five games, two more by extra time, making it seven in a row during these playoffs. In the finals, the Habs played Wayne Gretzky and the L.A. Kings, a team that had ruined the hopes of many Canadians longing for an Original Six matchup against Toronto, after defeating the Leafs in game seven at Maple Leaf Gardens.

The Kings won the opening game, 4-1, and then Roy again took control and won the next three games in overtime. They closed out the series, 4-1, in Montreal to win their 24th Cup. Roy again was named Conn Smythe winner. Incredibly, he did not record a single shutout in the 1993 playoffs, but he won a record ten straight overtime games, solidifying his place in the game's history as the greatest clutch goalie of the modern era.

Pete Peeters

For a goalie who played as well as Pete Peeters played, he had an awfully tough time getting the respect he thought he deserved. In the beginning, he deserved no respect at all. Drafted 135th overall by Philadelphia in 1977, he went to a team that wasn't even looking to acquire a goalie and even at that he was the 16th goalie selected in that year's draft. In short, not much was expected of him from the get-go.

Peeters was buoyed by being drafted at all, though, and turned pro right away. He started in the IHL and finished 1977-78 with Maine, the Flyers' farm team. The Mariners won the Calder Cup, and they won again the next year with Peeters in goal most of the season.

For 1979-80, he made the big team, but his role at training camp was to be backup to the newly-acquired Phil Myre who was replacing Bernie Parent. Parent was forced to retire because of an eye injury, but the Flyers didn't think for a second Peeters could be their main goalie. Quickly, though, he proved he could. In fact, he helped the Flyers play the first 35 games of the season without a loss, an NHL record that still stands, and his own undefeated streak reached 27 games before he lost for the first time that season—in February! The Flyers went to the Cup finals that year, but in the ensuing two seasons Peeters's GAA went up and the team's playoff performances went down.

To make matters worse, the Flyers had confidence in another goalie, Rick St. Croix, and they thought the goalie of the future was young Pelle Lindbergh. As a result, they eliminated the three-goalie worry from their agenda and traded Peeters to Boston in the summer of 1982. Peeters, though, vowed to prove to the Flyers they had made the wrong move. Indeed, he put together another mammoth undefeated streak with the Bruins in '82-'83, going 31 games without a loss and missing Gerry Cheevers' team and league record by just one game.

Still, this was his finest year. He led the NHL in wins (40), shutouts (eight), and GAA (2.36), and he took the team to the semi-finals of the playoffs before losing to the Cup-winning New York Islanders. He also led Team Canada to victory in the 1984 Canada Cup prior to the start of the new season. Peeters played in both the 1983 and 1984 All-Star Games, surrendering a respectable five goals in more than 60 minutes of play in games deminated by scorers.

Again, though, years two and three with the Bruins were slightly but progressively weaker and he was traded, this time to Washington. He had a lesser role with the Capitals, playing about 35 games a year for four years, but the team had little playoff success. Peeters finished his career back in Philadelphia, playing briefly for two years (1989-91) but producing a terrible record of 10-20-6 in that time.

Peter Skudra

By the time he made his first NHL appearance, November 5, 1997, for Pittsburgh against Dallas, goalie Peter Skudra had seen plenty of the hockey world. He grew up in Riga, Latvia, but that meant two very different things. Up to 1991 or so, Riga was part of Russia. After the fall of the Soviet empire, it meant Riga, Latvia. As a result, Skudra was the first of a new wave of Latvian players to appear internationally for the small, talented, and proud country.

In 1993 and 1994, he was on the national team that competed at the World Championship, B pool, and when Latvia advanced to the top pool he again played, in 1997 as backup to his hero, the legendary Arturs Irbe.

In between, Skudra played for a plethora of minor-league teams in the East Coast league, American league, and Central league. He was never drafted into the NHL, and when the Pittsburgh Penguins were looking for a backup to Tom Barrasso in '97-'98, they signed the 24-year-old veteran to a three-year deal. Although he spent much of that year in the minors again, Skudra performed well when asked. He finished with a record of 6-4-3 in 17 games and a fine 1.83 GAA with Pittsburgh. The next year, he virtually split the games with Barrasso, playing a career-high 37 times. His record of 15-11-5 was augmented by three shutouts (two against Toronto) and a 2.79 GAA, but the next year he slipped and the Penguins let him go in favour of Jean-Sebastien Aubin.

Buffalo signed him, waived him to Boston, and the Bruins released him, all in the same season. While he was respected as a solid goalie, he also established and then re-confirmed over and over his penchant for giving up soft goals at the worst time. Skudra's last NHL days passed with Vancouver where he was backup for two years (2001-03) behind Dan Cloutier, a role previously given to Martin Brochu who failed to take advantage of the opportunity. But despite having a winning record, Skudra did not set himself apart from Cloutier, let alone Brochu, whom the Canucks pegged as their playoff goalie.

Skudra heeded the signs and returned home where he played in the Russian Professional League, first with AK Bars Kazan and then Voskresensk where he became, for the first time in his career, the number-one man.

Philadelphia vs. Edmonton

After beating the New York Islanders in 1984 to claim their first Stanley Cup and end the Isles' reign at four Cups, the Edmonton Oilers were clearly the best team for the rest of the decade. There were, however, several teams vying to knock them off their top perch, and the title of second-best team might have gone to Boston, Calgary, or Philadelphia.

The most compelling rivalry, of course, was with Calgary, but because the two teams played in the same division and conference they could never meet in the finals. What a shame! It was, after all, the Flames that eventually won the Cup in 1986 to end the Oilers' two straight championships, a victory that has greater importance historically than at the time because Edmonton went on to win two more in a row. Thus, that '86 loss interrupted what might have been a five-Cup dynasty, achieved only once before in NHL history (Montreal, 1955-60).

To make matters worse, that loss was primarily the result of a pass by defenceman Steve Smith across his goalie's crease that banked off Grant Fuhr and into the net. While Smith is usually portrayed as the villain, it must be remembered that Fuhr was not following the play closely, either.

Nonetheless, the Oilers played Boston and Philadelphia twice each in the finals, winning all four series. The two meetings against the Bruins, though, were anticlimactic, the Oilers winning in four straight (with the suspended game thrown in for good measure) in 1988 and in five, uneventful games two years later.

Indeed, it was the Flyers that came closest to winning a Cup during these dominating years by the Oilers. They lost in five games in 1985 in a series in which the Oilers grew stronger every game. The Flyers won the first game, 4-1, but the Oilers, led by Wayne Gretzky, pulled away. Gretzky was held without a point in that loss, but over the next four games he scored seven times and added four assists to carry the team to victory and win the Conn Smythe Trophy for good measure. His *pièce de résistance* was the final game, won 8-3 by Edmonton, in which he scored twice and added two assists in the Cup-winning romp.

The Flyers had their best chance in 1987, thanks in large part to their rookie goalie, the sensational and controversial Ron Hextall. Nevertheless, the Oilers won game seven by a 3-1 score to win for the third time of the decade, a victory that had many shades to it. For starters, despite Hextall, his counterpart at the other end, Grant Fuhr, played even better. Despite scoring more goals than the Flyers, the Oilers were, surprisingly, the better team defensively as well. The Oilers also had many more weapons on the attack, starting with Gretzky but continuing with Jari Kurri, Glenn Anderson, and Mark Messier. The Flyers had only Rick Tocchet and Brian Propp to look to for goals consistently. And, the Oilers were every bit as big and tough as the Flyers.

In the end, it was Philadelphia's inability to contain Gretzky that was the difference. When the Islanders beat Edmonton in 1983 to win their fourth Cup in a row, they held Gretzky goalless in the four-game sweep, an unfathomable accomplishment that in itself could have led to victory. The Flyers could do no such thing. Of the 22 goals the Oilers scored in the finals, Gretzky was in on half of them (two goals, nine assists). As such, the Flyers earned the right to be called the second-best team of the post-Islanders '80s, small consolation, no doubt.

Phil Bourque

The good news was that Phil Bourque was, indeed, the brother of Ray Bourque of Boston. The bad news for hockey scouts was that this Ray Bourque was a native of that city and unrelated to the Hall of Fame defencemen who patrolled the Bruins' blueline for so many years.

Nonetheless, the career of Phil Bourque was all about perseverance. The native of Chelmsford, Massachusetts was never drafted but still moved north of the border to Kingston to play junior hockey for the Canadians in the OHL. The Pittsburgh Penguins signed him in 1982, and for the next ten years he was part of that team. However, the first half of that decade passed almost entirely in the minors for Bourque.

It wasn't until 1988, just 52 NHL games under his belt to that point, that he signed a proper, three-year contract with the Penguins that would reward him for his devotion and dedication. The Hockey Hall of Fame has in its possession this contract which is a study in player bonuses. The contract calls for standard payments of $150,000 for the first year and $160,000 for the next two years. But, appended to this standard contract is a separate sheet with 29 bonus clauses.

Bourque, for instance, would receive an extra $2,500 for being among the top three players in plus/minus on the team, provided he played at least 40 regular-season games. He received $1,000 for every shutout the team recorded, provided he played in the game. He even got an additional $500 for every game in which the team allowed one goal, provided he played in the game and the team won or tied the game. In other words, a 1-0 loss meant nada for his bank account.

He got an additional $1,500 if he scored 15 goals and 35 points during the season, which he did (17 goals, 43 points), but he failed to cash in on the next level which called for $2,500 with 20 goals and 45 points.

If the Penguins finished with the best penalty-killing record in their division, Bourque got an extra $2,500, and the Jennings Trophy standings also meant something: to win the trophy meant $3,000; to finish second, $2,000, and third $1,000.

There was also what can only be considered a miracle clause which called for Bourque to receive $10,000 if he won Conn Smythe Trophy as playoff MVP or the Lester B. Pearson Award as best player during the regular season as voted on by the players themselves. In this the era of Gretzky, Lemieux, Yzerman, and Hull, Phil Bourque's agent could have asked for a million dollars for same and the team would have been on safe footing accepting.

More realistically, Bourque got a bonus of $7,500 if the team won the Stanley Cup and he played at least two games. He cashed in twice on this, in 1991 and 1992. He failed to collect an another $25,000 for being named to the First All-Star Team, but by the time all was said and done he scored a few extra bucks on a contract he worked years to win.

Still, the Penguins let him go after the '92 Cup win and he signed with the Rangers and Ottawa before going down to the IHL and then across the ocean to Europe to finish his career. Not a bad life for a player no one wanted at 18 when he was draft eligible.

Pittsburgh Penguins 1991

The Pittsburgh Penguins started building for a Stanley Cup on a summer's day in 1984 when they drafted Mario Lemieux. The most talented 18-year-old to come out of Quebec junior hockey, Le Magnifique entered the NHL as a teen, scored a goal on his first shift, and never looked back.

A Cup is won not by any one player, however, but by a team. Despite having a sensational rookie season, Mario could not get the Penguins into the 1985 playoffs. Ditto in 1986 and 1987. Despite his incredible performance in September 1987 with Team Canada in the Canada Cup, 1987-88 saw the Pens miss the playoffs again despite his league best 70 goals and 168 points.

It wasn't until 1989, at the end of his fifth season, that Pittsburgh finally made it to the playoffs. The team swept the Rangers in the opening round before falling to Philadelphia in seven games the next round, but in 1990 the Penguins suffered a severe hiccough when they missed the playoffs again. In 1991, everything came together. First, coach Scotty Bowman was behind the bench and he knew better than anyone how to coach a player of Lemieux's talent.

Second, by this time general manager Craig Patrick had assembled a fine supporting cast for Mario, starting with goaltender Tom Barrasso. There was also Paul Coffey on defence, and the forwards were loaded with talent—Ron Francis, rookie Jaromir Jagr, Joe Mullen, Kevin Stevens, Mark Recchi, and Bryan Trottier.

The Penguins made it to the finals comfortably after beating New Jersey 4-0 in game seven of the opening round. They beat Washington in five games and Boston in six to face Minnesota in the finals, coached by Bob Gainey and managed by Bobby Clarke.

Lemieux and company were too strong, though. Super Mario scored in all five of the final games he played. He missed game three because of a muscle spasm in his back, a game the North Stars won, 3-1. Although he missed only the one game, there was panic in the Pittsburgh dressing room at this point because Lemieux had missed more than half the season (52 games, to be exact) because of back problems. That game actually gave the Stars a 2-1 series lead, but when Lemieux returned he dominated in a way few players have at this critical stage of the Cup showdown.

Although the Penguins got stronger as the series went on, they were aided by smart coaching, too. The key to the Stars was their two fastest players, forward Neal Broten and defenceman Mark Tinordi. By focusing on those players, coach Bowman nullified that speed, forced turnovers, and allowed Lemieux to have the puck more often.

The crushing blow was a powerful 8-0 whitewash in the clinching game, game six, in which Lemieux scored one goal short-handed and assisted on three others. It was the most lopsided NHL Cup-winning game in the trophy's long history. The game was played in Minnesota, and when the Penguins arrived home in the middle of the night they were greeted by 40,000 revellers at the airport, among them Pittsburgh Pirates MVP outfielder Barry Bonds and his wife.

Rendez-vous '87

The NHL learned its lesson from 1979. That year, it replaced the All-Star Game with a three-game series pitting a team of NHL all-stars against the best from the Soviet Union. After winning the first game 4-2, the NHLers lost game two 5-4 and were humiliated 6-0 in the deciding game, the more polished Soviets easily handling a team that had never played together before.

In 1987, Rendez-vous in Quebec City was another event to replace the All-Star Game, but this time it was a two-game series. The NHL team won the first game, 4-3, and lost the final game, 5-3. Unlike 1979, though, both these games were extraordinarily entertaining.

The NHL team had Gretzky and Lemieux at the height of their powers. The Soviets had the famed KLM line of Vladimir Krutov, Igor Larionov, and Sergei Makarov at the height of their powers. Grant Fuhr and Evgeni Belosheikan were the goalies at either end. The Edmonton Oilers had seven players on the NHL roster (an eighth, Paul Coffey, missed the series because of injury) while the Soviets had 12 members of the Red Army and six players from Moscow Dynamo.

The NHLers were the more tenacious and smarter in the first game. Coach Jean Perron had defencemen Rod Langway and Rick Green on the ice every time the KLM trio emerged. The Oilers threesome of Gretzky-Jari Kurri-Esa Tikkanen got the NHL off on the right foot with a goal early in the first period, and Glenn Anderson made it 2-0 late in the second.

The Soviets got on the board at 18:42, though, thanks to Alexei Kasatonov, and they tied the game early in the third. After exchanging goals midway through the period, Dave Poulin provided the heroics by scoring the winning goal with just 1:15 left in the third period. Much to the dismay of the fans, Soviet coach Viktor Tikhonov refused to pull his goalie in the final minute to try to tie the score, fearing, as always, he would be scored upon.

Game two started out the same, the NHL scoring early in the first and carrying a 1-0 lead to the dressing room. This time, though, the Soviets came out flying in the second period, scoring three unanswered goals and coasting to victory. It was a hard-hitting game, and perhaps to the surprise of the NHL, the Soviets matched the NHLers hit for hit. It was also a wide-open game, up-and-down action, great scoring chance one after the other. It was classic hockey.

After the game, Gretzky exchanged sweaters with Slava Fetisov, who would one day play many games in the NHL and win his share of Stanley Cups. Gretzky summed up the experience, though, with a public proposal for another Summit Series featuring a new generation of players. The showdown, of course, never materialized. "Let's face it," he said, "people want more than two games. And they want more than Christmas tours. And when it comes to the Canada Cup, who really wants to see Canada play West Germany? People want to see Canada and Russia. I'd like to see it happen before I retire."

Ron Hextall

He didn't win the Calder Trophy—Luc Robitaille did—but he did win the Vezina Trophy and the Conn Smythe Trophy, and missed the Jennings Trophy on the final night of the regular season. Not a bad way for a 23-year-old goalie to begin an NHL career.

Ron Hextall came from hockey blood. His father, uncle, and grandfather all played in the NHL, and Ron was the first true "third defenceman" in league history. Of course, he made his living stopping the puck, but he made his reputation in other ways. He was hands down the best puckhandler of goalies, setting a team record in Philadelphia with six assists in his first year. From the moment he entered the league, he talked about scoring a goal. He boasted of his ability to shoot the puck into the goal in the air from one end to the other, and he vowed that some night when the Flyers had a two-goal advantage and an empty net, he'd fire it home (he did, just not as a rookie). He was also tough as nails, setting records in both his first and second season for most penalty minutes by a goalie in a season and, amazingly, a career.

By the early part of the 1986-87 season, it was clear he was the number-one goalie according to coach Mike Keenan and GM Bobby Clarke. It was a promotion for the youngster thanks to the horrible accident to Pelle Lindbergh in which the goalie died from injuries in a car crash. Hextall came to the team and played like a starter right from training camp. He led the league in games played (66), wins (37), and minutes played (3,799). More important, he took the Flyers to the Stanley Cup finals to face the Edmonton Oilers, the league's most dominant team.

The Oilers were so conscious of Hextall that they abandoned shooting the puck hard into the Flyers' end. Instead, they flipped it softly to Hextall's backhand side so he wouldn't have time to move the puck up ice on his own. They also took advantage of his major weakness. While he came out well and played the puck like a defenceman, he was also caught out of his goal often and moved around his crease without body discipline. So, Wayne Gretzky made a point of setting up behind Hextall's net and moving the puck out in front this way, giving Hextall little time to react properly. The Oilers also knew that those penalty minutes the goalie accrued were in part because of a short fuse, so they disrupted him every chance they got with timely chops, slashes, and pokes.

Hextall was the main reason the Flyers got the finals, and he was the main reason those finals were extended to seven games. Game 1 was tied 2-2 after the second period before the Oilers exploded for three goals to win, 4-2. Game 2 went to overtime before the Oilers won again, 3-2. The Flyers won Game 3 by limiting Gretzky to a single assist. After Edmonton won Game 4 to take a 3-1 series lead and seemed to have the series in control, Hextall played his best. He also earned an eight-game suspension to start the next year after a vicious slash to Kent Nilsson's arm. In Games 5 and 6, the Oilers twice jumped into 2-0 leads, but Hextall refused to allow the next goal and the Flyers won both games to tie the series and force a deciding game. The Oilers won that game, 3-1, but they also outshot Philadelphia 43-20. The game was close only because of Hextall who earned scorn for the slash in Game 4 and praise for his superb rookie season.

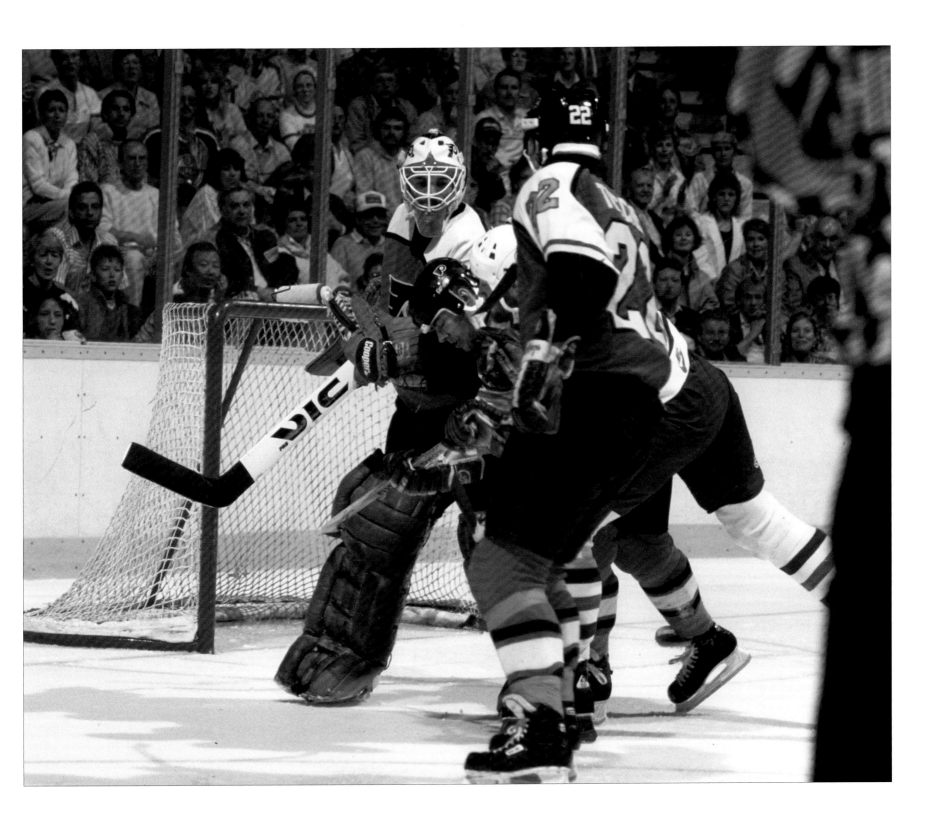

Russ Courtnall

Behind the success of Russ Courtnall are family pain and a close family bond with his brother, Geoff, who also skated for many years in the NHL, Bruce, who never played pro, and sister, Cheryl. Their uncle, Jim, drowned in 1975 in Oak Bay marina in British Columbia, and three years later their father, Archie, committed suicide at age 45 during a prolonged and painful depression. Russ was just 13 at the time.

Archie usually coached the boys' teams when they were kids, he himself having been good enough to attend a Detroit Red Wings training camp one year. Every Saturday night while they watched *Hockey Night in Canada*, he insisted they stand for *O Canada*. After Russ's dad died, his mom had to work because even at the best of times they were a poor more than well-off family. Notre Dame College in Wilcox, Saskatchewan, now named Athol Murray College in honour of its founder, called and invited Russ to attend the school and play hockey. He declined because of lack of funds. They insisted and provided a bursary.

The coach at Notre Dame was Barry MacKenzie, who played for the National Team in the 1960s, and he revived the spirit of Courtnall and instilled in him the desire to play that had been missing during the last year of his father's life. Russ went on to play junior in Victoria where he developed into one of the top prospects in the country. His teammates at Notre Dame included Wendel Clark and Gary Leeman, two other teens destined to play for the Leafs. Speed and skill were Courtnall's forte moreso than size and physical ability, and in 1983 the Leafs drafted him 7th overall.

Courtnall had a great season in '83-'84, playing first at the World Junior Championships and then a month later for Canada at the Olympics. He joined the Leafs at the end of that season, and never looked back. Nine times he scored 20 goals, and by the time he retired in 1999, he had 1,029 games to his credit. Geoff played a few more games (1,048, to be exact), but the only time the brothers played together was in Vancouver for 13 games in 1994-95. Geoff won one Stanley Cup with Edmonton in 1988, and the next year Russ came close with Montreal before losing to Calgary in the finals.

Despite playing in Toronto, Montreal, and Los Angeles during his career, Russ moved home after his playing days where he and his California wife raised their three children. His purpose became all the clearer when he read about the local hospital, Royal Jubilee, and its need for a new psychiatric emergency unit. Of course, this struck close to home because of his father, so in 2001 he and Geoff, who lived just a few blocks away, organized the Courtnall Classic, an annual summer golf tournament to raise funds for the new unit. The event was such a success that even after it was built, they continued to host the charity event to raise money for other local causes.

While some players live in the city where their careers end or where they spent the majority of their careers, others, like the Courtnalls, return home. For Russ, it was a return to a place of comfort and sadness, but a place that is the only home he ever knew.

Shayne Corson

The career of Shayne Corson was a fine one, to be sure, but most people in hockey are left wondering what might have been had the same talent been put inside a different personality.

The Barrie native played junior in Hamilton with a style that was all his own. He could score and pass, skate and check, and he could fight to create more room for himself. Montreal thought so highly of him that it drafted him 8th overall in 1984, and a year and a half later he made his NHL debut and never looked back.

As he learned to play in the NHL, Corson looked to fighting first as a way of establishing himself. It was easier than scoring, and he believed by becoming known as a tough player he could earn the respect of team-mates and foes alike. His strategy worked, and within three years he scored 26 goals and then 31 to leave his mark on the scoreboard as well as penalty box. He played for Team Canada in the victorious 1991 Canada Cup as well, a learning experience for the young star. But before fans and coaches could admire him for his development, he was getting into trouble off ice that threatened his career and reputation.

Montreal gave up on him after the '91-'92 season just one year after signing him to a large, new contract. He had just finished a disappointing season in which he managed just 17 goals, and in ten playoff games he contributed only two more. The Habs traded him to Edmonton, but he had trouble adjusting. Like his early years, he didn't score so much as spend plenty of time in the penalty box. That first year with the Oilers was a wakeup call for Corson, and he responded accordingly. In his second season, he had 25 goals and halved his penalty minutes total, taking on a greater leadership role with the young Oilers.

He played one more year in Edmonton, the lockout-shortened 1994-95 season, and then moved to St. Louis where he signed as a free agent. After a year and a half playing out of the spotlight of a Canadian city, Corson earned his way back to the Canadiens in '97-'98 where he was traded mid-season. Corson had a good enough season and had improved his reputation to the point that Team Canada general manager Bobby Clarke named Corson to the Olympic team for Canada in Nagano in 1998, the first time NHL players would participate en masse at the Olympics. Corson had a good tournament, but the team returned disappointed by a fourth-place finish.

Corson played two more uneven seasons before landing in Toronto with his brother-in-law, Darcy Tucker, and for two years the pair played gritty, admirable hockey and the Leafs had decent runs in the playoffs to make the signing look smart. During the playoffs in 2003, however, Corson suddenly left the team, retiring from hockey altogether. He blamed a series of panic attacks as well as his inability to control a colitis problem he had fought since a teen. After almost a year off, he was signed by Dallas in an attempt to return to the game, but at season's end his career was over. In all, he played an impressive 1,156 games and scored 273 goals, but somewhere deep inside him there was probably more than those numbers gave out.

Theo Fleury

Before his various moments of lost composure with the New York Rangers, Chicago Blackhawks, Horse Lake Thunder, and Belfast Giants, Theo Fleury established a reputation as the greatest under-sized player of the modern era. Small but determined, short but fiery, he was a great scorer, a physical player, and a leader who helped take Calgary to the Stanley Cup in 1989, his rookie season. He has been described using the same set of Homeric epithets: little big man, tenacious, sparkplug, unrelenting, determined, fighter in every sense of the word.

As a child, he was raised by a father who was alcoholic and a mother who was addicted to prescription drugs. As a young teen, he was coached by Graham James who was later jailed for sexually abusing teammate Sheldon Kennedy. Yet playing for the Moose Jaw Warriors in the WHL, Fleury scored a goal a game his last two years and averaged almost three points a game. He also accumulated 345 penalty minutes in that same time.

The only problem was that he stood just 5'5" and every scout on the planet believed he would be too small to adjust in the NHL. Accordingly, he was drafted a lowly 166th overall in 1987 by Calgary. A few months earlier, he was on the Team Canada team that was disqualified from the World Junior Championship for brawling with the Soviets. After that game, Fleury vowed to win gold the next year. He captained the 1988 junior team to that promised victory and the succeeding year he started his pro career in Salt Lake, Calgary's IHL affiliate.

Fleury was called up to the Flames midway through the '88-'89 season and never looked back. In his first full season he scored 31 goals; in his second year, he upped that to 51. Although it was his only year to reach the half century mark, Fleury became a guaranteed 30-goal scorer. He ended his career with 455 goals and 1,088 total points, an amazing career for someone 5'5" in a league that accentuated size and strength.

Fleury had a mean streak that, combined with sharpened survival skills, made him something of a loose cannon and feared opponent. He also had a great shot and fearless approach to the corners and front of the net where puck battles were played out and goals scored.

Fleury was fiercely proud to be Canadian. He proved his value on the international stage at the 1988 World Juniors, and proved it time and again thereafter. When the Flames were eliminated early from the 1990 and '91 playoffs, he accepted invitations to play for Canada at the senior World Championships. He played on the champion Team Canada at the 1991 Canada Cup and was one of the best players in 1996 at the World Cup. Fleury was in tears when he was named to Canada's '98 Olympic team, the first time the NHL went to the games, but perhaps his crowning moment came in 2002 when he helped Canada to gold at the Salt Lake Olympics.

After an horrific first year on Broadway in 2000-01, in which he entered the league's substance-abuse program, Fleury behaved himself off ice and excelled on it. His blistering start to '01-'02, and his new attitude, made him an obvious choice for the team, and through the tournament he was on his best behaviour. On ice, he played with skill and discipline. Canada won gold. Theo was an Olympic champion.

Toronto vs. New Jersey 2001

Since the early 1990s the Leafs have been a consistent playoff team and have come tantalizingly close to a visit to the Stanley Cup finals, something they have not done since 1967 when they last won the trophy. They had tremendous runs through the post-season in 1993 and 1994 when they went to the Conference finals, led by Doug Gilmour, and more recently they had a close call in 1999 when they went as far, only to lose to Buffalo in five games.

In 2001, they had another excellent team but couldn't get past New Jersey in the Conference semi-finals. Game 2 on April 28, 2001 (pictured here), was one of the vintage games Mats Sundin ever played in a Leafs sweater, but as was so often the case, his performance was not enough.

Sundin assisted on a first-period goal by defenceman Danny Markov, but in the second period the Devils exploded for four goals to take a commanding 4-1 lead after 40 minutes. Alexander Mogilny was the hero for the Devils, scoring one of those four and assisting on the other three.

Sundin, though, got the team right back into the game just 29 seconds into the third, scoring a short-handed goal which was the team's first such goal on the road all season. New Jersey struck right back, though, when Mogilny scored again on that same power play, his fifth point of the night, and now the score was 5-2.

Sundin refused to give up. He set up Steve Thomas for a goal a few minutes later, and then scored again while the teams were 5-on-5 midway through the period. The Leafs continued to press, and in the final minute they got what they wanted. With Curtis Joseph on the bench, Sundin brought the puck in over the New Jersey line. Bobby Holik took it from him, but as he tried to ice it Steve Thomas picked the puck out of midair in the slot, put it down on the ice quickly, and rifled a shot home to tie the game 5-5 at 19:37. It was a terrific comeback, but it fell just short. Randy MacKay scored 5:31 into the overtime, converting a 2-on-1 with Holik.

The Leafs lost the next game at home, 3-2 in overtime, and then reeled off consecutive victories of 3-1 and 3-2 to take a 3-2 lead in the series. Game six, at the Air Canada Centre, though, proved a disappointment. Instead of eliminating the Devils, they lost 4-2, and game seven, back at the Meadowlands was all New Jersey and the Devils won, 5-1.

The next year, the Leafs came closest yet, perhaps, to reaching the finals. They advanced to the Conference finals only to lose to Carolina on home ice in a dramatic game seven thanks to a giveaway by that same Mogilny, who signed with the Leafs the previous summer, deep in his own end. In 2003, the Leafs were eliminated by Philadelphia in the first round in seven games, and the year after sent packing by the Flyers again, this time in the second round. In 2005, there were no playoffs, and in '06 the Leafs failed to qualify for the post-season for the first time under Pat Quinn. Quinn lost his job, and the Leafs remained no closer to a modern Cup win than with these more recent near misses.

Vancouver Canucks Sweaters

Perhaps no team has made more significant changes to their sweater than the Canucks, and if popular opinion counts, as it should, most of those changes have been for the worse.

When the team entered the NHL in 1970 it sported a perfectly excellent design. The rink-shaped logo featured green outline and blue inside to designate the ice. A white stick ran through the rink from the right side. It was a simple yet colourful logo, but by 1978 the powers that be in the organization decided to make a radical change to the design.

The modern logo of the day that year featured a round shape with orange outline and the word CANUCKS slashed through the bottom of it. Above this was a stylized skate made up of a series of yellow and red lines. This lasted all of one year after a poor reception, and the team again made a radical alteration to the logo.

The third version was likely the ugliest of all. It featured a series of V-shapes starting at the shoulders and meeting at the waist. The colours were orange, yellow, and black and resembled no other sweater that had passed through the league. It also was disliked by fans, but it stayed in circulation for five years. In 1984, the team reverted to the round logo with the multi-coloured skate.

Another change took place in the summer of 1997, a few months after Orca Entertainment acquired majority ownership of the team. The latest, and current, edition featured a blue "C" (representing Canucks) out of which burst an orca whale. On the shoulders is a variation of the original logo, but the green border is now red and the light blue ice now dark blue.

Ironically, the Canucks have also adopted a third sweater—the original one from 1970! Just as everything old is new again, so the fans' desire to embrace nostalgia has made the logo, which executives said had become staid and tired, in vogue. In fact, the third version today is the most popular sweater of the team, which now perhaps realizes that the best logo of all was the one that perhaps should never have changed—the original!

The Canucks are by no means the only team to tamper with their original togs, though. Virtually every team in the last generation has altered its sweater somehow. In traditional cities such as Toronto, Montreal, and Detroit, those changes can mean simply adding an extra colour (silver, to the Leafs' lettering), or making the logo a bit bigger (as is the case with the vaunted "C H" of Montreal and the Winged Wheel of the Red Wings).

Other Original Six teams and less traditional teams alike have made more of an overhaul. The Bruins, Rangers, and Islanders all have third sweaters that don't hearken back but re-interpret the team's place in the city, to negative effect, by fans' reactions. Fans have indicated time and again that the old or the original, the pure and untampered, is their favourite sweater design.

Edmonton vs. Islanders

Great as the Edmonton Oilers became in the 1980s, they learned their lessons long and hard in losing before they discovered the secret to winning. That secret lay not in some magic potion or some special prayer but in hard work, tenacity, and a willingness to skate through walls to win.

The Oilers learned their greatest lesson courtesy of the Islanders, the great team that began the 1980s with four straight Stanley Cup victories, the last of which was a four-game sweep of the Oilers in 1983. How did they beat the highest-scoring team in NHL history four games in a row? How did they hold that offense to a meagre six goals? How did they prevent Gretzky from putting the puck in the net even once? Not luck—hard work. And, superior play.

Game one, in Edmonton, sent the message loud and clear as the Islanders won 2-0 on a Billy Smith shutout. The Oilers had 35 shots but couldn't beat "Battlin' Billy," and psychologically the damage was worse than the score. Further, in that game Smith slashed Edmonton forward Glenn Anderson near the crease, sending a clear message that he was not to be trifled with. After, coach Glen Sather heaped scorn on the enemy goalie and called for a suspension, but Smith had done his job by throwing the Oilers off their game.

Game two was a repeat performance but with more hysterics and histrionics. The Islanders dominated again and were cruising to a 6-3 victory when, late in the third period, Gretzky came out from behind the New York net. Smith swung his stick loosely behind him, catching Gretzky on the knee. The Great One fell to the ice in agony, and Smith drew a five-minute major penalty. Later, Dave Lumley answered back by spearing Smith. The war was on, which was fine by the Islanders. Anything but let Edmonton think about scoring, was their philosophy.

Games three and four on Long Island provided more Smith lore. In the former, he stoned the Oilers for two periods while the players in front of him withstood a ferocious Edmonton attack, and in the third they took a 1-1 game and turned it into a 5-1 victory. Smith was the hero, but Gretzky, now goalless in three games, was for the first time in his career vulnerable to criticism for not having what it takes to play in the big games.

In game four, the Oilers simply couldn't match the Islanders in intensity and desire. The New Yorkers jumped into a 3-0 lead after 20 minutes, but although the Oilers scored the only two goals of the second, that was as close as they came. New York added an insurance goal in the third and won their 16th consecutive playoff series in dominating fashion. Billy Smith was named Conn Smythe Trophy winner, and Gretzky left the building having not scored in four straight games, an incredible achievement by the Islanders in shutting down the player who scored 83 times in 92 games heading into the finals (regular season and playoffs combined).

As the pretty-boy Oilers left the Nassau Coliseum victims of a sweep, Gretzky and friends passed by the New York dressing room and saw not a bunch of champagne-drunk players whooping it up. Instead, they saw a bunch of men in pain, exhausted, ready for a bus trip to the local hospital more than a downtown bar. The Oilers learned then what it takes to win.

Acknowledgements

The author would like to thank the many people whose contributions, support, and friendship have made this book possible. First, to publisher Jordan Fenn for his continued and exceptional enthusiasm for such projects, and to designer Kathryn Del Borrello for taking the raw material and making it look special. To everyone at the Hockey Hall of Fame: Bill Hay, Jeff Denomme, Phil Pritchard, Craig Baines, Craig Campbell, Peter Jagla, Darren Boyko, Kelly Masse, Ron Ellis, Izak Westegate, Kevin Shea, Anthony Fusco, Marilyn Robbins, Miragh Addis, Danielle Siciliano, Steve Ozimec, Steve Poirier, Jackie Schwartz, Pearl Rajwanth, Craig Beckim, Patrick Minogue, Dave Stubbs, Sylvia Lau, Wendy Cramer, Sandra Walters, Matt Mitanis, Scott Veber, Mike Akilu, Mike Briggs, Tome Geneski, Joanne Laird, Stephanie Lui, and, of course, the one and only Tyler Wolosewich. Specific thanks are due to Craig Campbell for coordinating the project, Kevin Shea for editing, and Phil Pritchard for managing everything. Thanks also to agent Dean Cooke and associate Suzanne Brandreth. And, lastly, to family—mom, Liz, Ian, Zachary, Emily, and Mary Jane, whose feelings toward hockey are, well, difficult to put into words.